THIS DIARY BELONGS TO:

Name: Phone: Mobile:

Address:

Email:

Emergency Contact: Phone: Mobile:

GP: Phone:

COMPANY / SERVICE

Business Name:

Phone: Mobile: Fax:

Address:

PO Box:

Email:

Website:

Facebook Page: Twitter:

Skype ID: Other IM:

Business Number: Licence:

EMPLOYER DETAILS

Name: Phone: Mobile:

Email:

Address:

PERSONAL RECORDS

Car Registration: Tax File Number:

Medical: Blood Type:

Anniversaries: name: date:

Anniversaries: name: date:

Anniversaries: name: date:

LOGINS (do not store privacy or financial logins here)

website:	username/login:	password:
website:	username/login:	password:
website:	username/login:	password:
website:	username/login:	password:
website:	username/login:	password:
website:	username/login:	password:
website:	username/login:	password:

© Butler Diaries Pty Ltd

EMERGENCY CALL _____

Perpetual Year Planner

JANUARY	FEBRUARY	MARCH	APRIL	MAY	JUNE
1	1	1	1	1	1
2	2	2	2	2	2
3	3	3	3	3	3
4	4	4	4	4	4
5	5	5	5	5	5
6	6	6	6	6	6
7	7	7	7	7	7
8	8	8	8	8	8
9	9	9	9	9	9
10	10	10	10	10	10
11	11	11	11	11	11
12	12	12	12	12	12
13	13	13	13	13	13
14	14	14	14	14	14
15	15	15	15	15	15
16	16	16	16	16	16
17	17	17	17	17	17
18	18	18	18	18	18
19	19	19	19	19	19
20	20	20	20	20	20
21	21	21	21	21	21
22	22	22	22	22	22
23	23	23	23	23	23
24	24	24	24	24	24
25	25	25	25	25	25
26	26	26	26	26	26
27	27	27	27	27	27
28	28	28	28	28	28
29	29 (2024, 2028)	29	29	29	29
30		30	30	30	30
31		31		31	

© Butler Diaries Pty Ltd

JULY	AUGUST	SEPTEMBER	OCTOBER	NOVEMBER	DECEMBER
1	1	1	1	1	1
2	2	2	2	2	2
3	3	3	3	3	3
4	4	4	4	4	4
5	5	5	5	5	5
6	6	6	6	6	6
7	7	7	7	7	7
8	8	8	8	8	8
9	9	9	9	9	9
10	10	10	10	10	10
11	11	11	11	11	11
12	12	12	12	12	12
13	13	13	13	13	13
14	14	14	14	14	14
15	15	15	15	15	15
16	16	16	16	16	16
17	17	17	17	17	17
18	18	18	18	18	18
19	19	19	19	19	19
20	20	20	20	20	20
21	21	21	21	21	21
22	22	22	22	22	22
23	23	23	23	23	23
24	24	24	24	24	24
25	25	25	25	25	25
26	26	26	26	26	26
27	27	27	27	27	27
28	28	28	28	28	28
29	29	29	29	29	29
30	30	30	30	30	30
31	31		31		31
JULY	AUGUST	SEPTEMBER	OCTOBER	NOVEMBER	DECEMBER

© Butler Diaries Pty Ltd

TERM PLANNING OVERVIEW

TERM 1: Starting........................ Ending........................

W1	
W2	
W3	
W4	
W5	
W6	
W7	
W8	
W9	
W10	
W	
HOLS	
HOLS	

TERM 2: Starting........................ Ending........................

W1	
W2	
W3	
W4	
W5	
W6	
W7	
W8	
W9	
W10	
W	
HOLS	
HOLS	

TERM 3: Starting........................ Ending........................

W1	
W2	
W3	
W4	
W5	
W6	
W7	
W8	
W9	
W10	
W	
HOLS	
HOLS	

TERM 4: Starting........................ Ending........................

W1	
W2	
W3	
W4	
W5	
W6	
W7	
W8	
W9	
W10	
W	
HOLS	
HOLS	

© Butler Diaries Pty Ltd

Weekly Timetable Planners

TIME	MONDAY	TUESDAY	WEDNESDAY	THURSDAY	FRIDAY	SATURDAY	SUNDAY

© Butler Diaries Pty Ltd

TIME	MONDAY	TUESDAY	WEDNESDAY	THURSDAY	FRIDAY	SATURDAY	SUNDAY

© Butler Diaries Pty Ltd

Weekly Menu

Starting Monday: / /

		Monday	Tuesday	Wednesday	Thursday	Friday
Breakfast	Purees / semi-solid					
	Whole food and drink					
Morning Tea	Purees / semi-solid					
	Whole food and drink					
Lunch	Purees / semi-solid					
	Whole food and drink					
Afternoon Tea	Purees / semi-solid					
	Whole food and drink					
Late Afternoon Tea	Purees / semi-solid					
	Whole food and drink					
Dinner	Purees / semi-solid					
	Whole food and drink					

** Alternatives will be catered to for allergies/intolerance or cultural/religious reason. These will have been prearranged according to the individual child's alternative management plan.

© Butler Diaries Pty Ltd

Incident, Injury, Trauma and Illness Record

Type of record: ☐ Incident ☐ Injury ☐ Trauma ☐ Illness

DETAILS OF PERSON COMPLETING THIS RECORD

Name: .... Position/role: ....

Time record was made: .... am/pm Date: .... / .... / .... Signature: ....

CHILD DETAILS

Surname: .... Given names: ....

Date of birth: .... / .... / .... Age: .... Gender: .... Room/group: ....

INCIDENT / INJURY / TRAUMA / ILLNESS DETAILS

Location: .... Time: .... am/pm Date: .... / .... /

Name of witness: .... Signature: .... Date: .... / .... /

General activity and circumstances leading to the **incident/injury/trauma/illness**: ....
....
....

Circumstances surrounding any **illness** including apparent symptoms: ....
....
....

Circumstances if child appeared to be **missing** or otherwise unaccounted for (incl duration, who found child etc): ....
....
....

Circumstances if child appeared to have been **taken or removed** from service or was **locked in/out** of service (incl who took the child, duration):
....
....

Nature of injury/trauma/illness sustained: Indicate on diagram the part of body affected

☐ Abrasion / Scrape   ☐ Burn / sunburn   ☐ High temperature   ☐ Sprain / swelling
☐ Allergic reaction   ☐ Choking   ☐ Ingestion /inhalation   ☐ Stabbing / piercing
   (not anaphylaxis)   ☐ Concussion   / insertion   ☐ Tooth
☐ Amputation   ☐ Crush / jam   ☐ Internal injury /   ☐ Venomous bite/sting
☐ Anaphylaxis   ☐ Cut / open wound   Infection   ☐ Other (please specify)
☐ Asthma / respiratory   ☐ Drowning (non-fatal)   ☐ Poisoning   ....
☐ Bite wound   ☐ Electric shock   ☐ Rash   ....
☐ Bruise   ☐ Eye injury   ☐ Respiratory   ....
☐ Broken bone /dislocation   ☐ Infectious disease   ☐ Seizure /unconscious/
                                                           convulsion

ACTION TAKEN

Details of action taken, including first aid, administration of medication: ....
....
....

Medical Personnel or Emergency Services contacted: Yes / No   If yes, provide details: ....

NOTIFICATIONS (INCLUDING ATTEMPTED NOTIFICATIONS):

Parent/guardian .... Time: .... am/pm Date: ..../............/............

Director/educator/coordinator .... Time: .... am/pm Date: ..../............/............

Regulatory authority (if applicable) .... Time: .... am/pm Date: ..../............/............

PARENTAL ACKNOWLEDGEMENT:

I .... have been notified of my child's incident / injury / trauma / illness. (Please circle)
(name of parent/guardian)

Signature:... Date ..../............/............

Additional Notes /Follow Up:...
....
....
....

© Butter Diaries Pty Ltd

Administration of Medication Record

Child's name: **Date of birth:**   **Comments:**

To be completed by the parent/guardian							To be completed by the educator when administered						
Name of medication	Last administered		To be administered (or circumstances to be administered)		Dosage to be administered	Method of administration	Signature of parent/guardian	Medication administered	To be completed		Dosage administered	Method of administration	Name of person administering	Signature of person administering	Signature of witness (not required for FDC or Nanny)
	Time	Date	Time	Date					Time	Date					

© Butler Diaries Pty Ltd

Quality Improvement Goals

Clean and Check

Repair or Replace

Wish List to Buy

Update Records

To Do List

PROFESSIONAL DEVELOPMENT SUMMARY

DATE	PROFESSIONAL DEVELOPMENT ACTIVITY / WHO	PROVIDER	HOURS	COST	COMMENTS

MARK HOURS AS * FOR INTERNAL OR + FOR EXTERNAL

MONDAY	TUESDAY	WEDNESDAY	THURSDAY	FRIDAY	SATURDAY	SUNDAY
☑	☐	☐	☐	☐	☐	☐

Our Day

DATE: START TIME: FINISH:

Family Communication to Nanny / Educator

Notes to Family / Supplies Needed

Play Dates / Nanny Share

Menu / Bottles
Meal	Description / Time

Sleeps
Name: From: To:

☐ Check every 10 min

Expenses
Price	Description

Toileting / Nappies

Activities / Outings

SUNSCREEN ☐

Observations / Reflections

INITIAL

| MONDAY ☑ | TUESDAY ☐ | WEDNESDAY ☐ | THURSDAY ☐ | FRIDAY ☐ | SATURDAY ☐ | SUNDAY ☐ |

Our Day

DATE: START TIME: FINISH:

Family Communication to Nanny / Educator

Notes to Family / Supplies Needed

Play Dates / Nanny Share

Menu / Bottles

Meal	Description / Time

Sleeps

Name: From: To:

☐ Check every 10 min

Expenses

Price	Description

Toileting / Nappies

Activities / Outings

SUNSCREEN ☐

Observations / Reflections

INITIAL

© Butler Diaries

| MONDAY ☑ | TUESDAY ☐ | WEDNESDAY ☐ | THURSDAY ☐ | FRIDAY ☐ | SATURDAY ☐ | SUNDAY ☐ |

Our Day

DATE:　　　　　　　　START TIME:　　　　　　　　FINISH:

Family Communication to Nanny / Educator

Notes to Family / Supplies Needed

Play Dates / Nanny Share

Menu / Bottles
Meal	Description / Time

Sleeps
Name:　　From:　　To:

☐ Check every 10 min

Expenses
Price	Description

Toileting / Nappies

Activities / Outings

☐ SUNSCREEN

Observations / Reflections

INITIAL

© Butler Diaries

Our Day

MONDAY	TUESDAY	WEDNESDAY	THURSDAY	FRIDAY	SATURDAY	SUNDAY
☑	☐	☐	☐	☐	☐	☐

DATE: START TIME: FINISH:

Family Communication to Nanny / Educator

Notes to Family / Supplies Needed

Play Dates / Nanny Share

Menu / Bottles

Meal	Description / Time

Sleeps

Name: From: To:

☐ Check every 10 min

Expenses

Price	Description

Toileting / Nappies

Activities / Outings

SUNSCREEN ☐

Observations / Reflections

INITIAL

| MONDAY ☑ | TUESDAY ☐ | WEDNESDAY ☐ | THURSDAY ☐ | FRIDAY ☐ | SATURDAY ☐ | SUNDAY ☐ |

Our Day

DATE: START TIME: FINISH:

Family Communication to Nanny / Educator

Notes to Family / Supplies Needed

Play Dates / Nanny Share

Menu / Bottles
Meal	Description / Time

Sleeps
Name: From: To:

☐ Check every 10 min

Expenses
Price	Description

Toileting / Nappies

Activities / Outings

SUNSCREEN ☐

Observations / Reflections

INITIAL

| MONDAY ☑ | TUESDAY ☐ | WEDNESDAY ☐ | THURSDAY ☐ | FRIDAY ☐ | SATURDAY ☐ | SUNDAY ☐ |

Our Day

DATE: START TIME: FINISH:

Family Communication to Nanny / Educator

Notes to Family / Supplies Needed

Play Dates / Nanny Share

Menu / Bottles

Meal	Description / Time

Sleeps

Name: From: To:

☐ Check every 10 min

Expenses

Price	Description

Toileting / Nappies

Activities / Outings

SUNSCREEN ☐

Observations / Reflections

INITIAL

© Butter Diaries

| MONDAY ☑ | TUESDAY ☐ | WEDNESDAY ☐ | THURSDAY ☐ | FRIDAY ☐ | SATURDAY ☐ | SUNDAY ☐ |

Our Day

DATE: START TIME: FINISH:

Family Communication to Nanny / Educator

Notes to Family / Supplies Needed

Play Dates / Nanny Share

Menu / Bottles
Meal	Description / Time

Sleeps
Name: From: To:

☐ Check every 10 min

Expenses
Price	Description

Toileting / Nappies

Activities / Outings

SUNSCREEN ☐

Observations / Reflections

INITIAL

| MONDAY ☑ | TUESDAY ☐ | WEDNESDAY ☐ | THURSDAY ☐ | FRIDAY ☐ | SATURDAY ☐ | SUNDAY ☐ |

Our Day

DATE: START TIME: FINISH:

Family Communication to Nanny / Educator

Notes to Family / Supplies Needed

Play Dates / Nanny Share

Menu / Bottles

Meal	Description / Time

Sleeps

Name: From: To:

☐ Check every 10 min

Expenses

Price	Description

Toileting / Nappies

Activities / Outings

SUNSCREEN ☐

Observations / Reflections

INITIAL

© Butler Diaries

MONDAY ☑ TUESDAY ☐ WEDNESDAY ☐ THURSDAY ☐ FRIDAY ☐ SATURDAY ☐ SUNDAY ☐

Our Day

DATE: START TIME: FINISH:

Family Communication to Nanny / Educator

Notes to Family / Supplies Needed

Play Dates / Nanny Share

Menu / Bottles

Meal	Description / Time

Sleeps

Name: From: To:

☐ Check every 10 min

Expenses

Price	Description

Toileting / Nappies

Activities / Outings

☐ SUNSCREEN

Observations / Reflections

INITIAL

© Butler Diaries

MONDAY	TUESDAY	WEDNESDAY	THURSDAY	FRIDAY	SATURDAY	SUNDAY
☑	☐	☐	☐	☐	☐	☐

Our Day

DATE: START TIME: FINISH:

Family Communication to Nanny / Educator

Notes to Family / Supplies Needed

Play Dates / Nanny Share

Menu / Bottles

Meal	Description / Time

Sleeps

Name: From: To:

☐ Check every 10 min

Expenses

Price	Description

Toileting / Nappies

Activities / Outings

SUNSCREEN ☐

Observations / Reflections

INITIAL

Our Day

| MONDAY ☑ | TUESDAY ☐ | WEDNESDAY ☐ | THURSDAY ☐ | FRIDAY ☐ | SATURDAY ☐ | SUNDAY ☐ |

DATE: START TIME: FINISH:

Family Communication to Nanny / Educator

Notes to Family / Supplies Needed

Play Dates / Nanny Share

Menu / Bottles

Meal	Description / Time

Sleeps

Name: From: To:

☐ Check every 10 min

Expenses

Price	Description

Toileting / Nappies

Activities / Outings

SUNSCREEN ☐

Observations / Reflections

INITIAL

© Butter Diaries

| MONDAY ☑ | TUESDAY ☐ | WEDNESDAY ☐ | THURSDAY ☐ | FRIDAY ☐ | SATURDAY ☐ | SUNDAY ☐ |

Our Day

DATE: START TIME: FINISH:

Family Communication to Nanny / Educator

Notes to Family / Supplies Needed

Play Dates / Nanny Share

Menu / Bottles
Meal	Description / Time

Sleeps
Name: From: To:

☐ Check every 10 min

Expenses
Price	Description

Toileting / Nappies

Activities / Outings

SUNSCREEN ☐

Observations / Reflections

INITIAL

© Butler Diaries

MONDAY	TUESDAY	WEDNESDAY	THURSDAY	FRIDAY	SATURDAY	SUNDAY
☑	☐	☐	☐	☐	☐	☐

Our Day

DATE:	START TIME:	FINISH:

Family Communication to Nanny / Educator

Notes to Family / Supplies Needed

Play Dates / Nanny Share

Menu / Bottles

Meal	Description / Time

Sleeps

Name:	From:	To:

☐ Check every 10 min

Expenses

Price	Description

Toileting / Nappies

Activities / Outings

SUNSCREEN ☐

Observations / Reflections

INITIAL

Our Day

| MONDAY ☑ | TUESDAY ☐ | WEDNESDAY ☐ | THURSDAY ☐ | FRIDAY ☐ | SATURDAY ☐ | SUNDAY ☐ |

DATE: START TIME: FINISH:

Family Communication to Nanny / Educator

Notes to Family / Supplies Needed

Play Dates / Nanny Share

Menu / Bottles
Meal	Description / Time

Sleeps
Name: From: To:

☐ Check every 10 min

Expenses
Price	Description

Toileting / Nappies

Activities / Outings

SUNSCREEN ☐

Observations / Reflections

INITIAL

© Butler Diaries

Our Day

| MONDAY ☑ | TUESDAY ☐ | WEDNESDAY ☐ | THURSDAY ☐ | FRIDAY ☐ | SATURDAY ☐ | SUNDAY ☐ |

DATE:　　　　　START TIME:　　　　　FINISH:

Family Communication to Nanny / Educator

Notes to Family / Supplies Needed

Play Dates / Nanny Share

Menu / Bottles
Meal | Description / Time

Sleeps
Name:　From:　To:

☐ Check every 10 min

Expenses
Price | Description

Toileting / Nappies

Activities / Outings

SUNSCREEN ☐

Observations / Reflections

INITIAL

| MONDAY ☑ | TUESDAY ☐ | WEDNESDAY ☐ | THURSDAY ☐ | FRIDAY ☐ | SATURDAY ☐ | SUNDAY ☐ |

Our Day

DATE: START TIME: FINISH:

Family Communication to Nanny / Educator

Notes to Family / Supplies Needed

Play Dates / Nanny Share

Menu / Bottles

Meal	Description / Time

Sleeps

Name: From: To:

☐ Check every 10 min

Expenses

Price	Description

Toileting / Nappies

Activities / Outings

SUNSCREEN ☐

Observations / Reflections

INITIAL

© Butler Diaries

| MONDAY ☑ | TUESDAY ☐ | WEDNESDAY ☐ | THURSDAY ☐ | FRIDAY ☐ | SATURDAY ☐ | SUNDAY ☐ |

Our Day

DATE: START TIME: FINISH:

Family Communication to Nanny / Educator

Notes to Family / Supplies Needed

Play Dates / Nanny Share

Menu / Bottles

Meal	Description / Time

Sleeps

Name:	From:	To:

☐ Check every 10 min

Expenses

Price	Description

Toileting / Nappies

Activities / Outings

SUNSCREEN ☐

Observations / Reflections

INITIAL

Our Day

MONDAY	TUESDAY	WEDNESDAY	THURSDAY	FRIDAY	SATURDAY	SUNDAY
☑	☐	☐	☐	☐	☐	☐

DATE: START TIME: FINISH:

Family Communication to Nanny / Educator

Notes to Family / Supplies Needed

Play Dates / Nanny Share

Menu / Bottles

Meal	Description / Time

Sleeps

Name: From: To:

☐ Check every 10 min

Expenses

Price	Description

Toileting / Nappies

Activities / Outings

☐ SUNSCREEN

Observations / Reflections

INITIAL

© Butler Diaries

Our Day

| MONDAY ☑ | TUESDAY ☐ | WEDNESDAY ☐ | THURSDAY ☐ | FRIDAY ☐ | SATURDAY ☐ | SUNDAY ☐ |

DATE: START TIME: FINISH:

Family Communication to Nanny / Educator

Notes to Family / Supplies Needed

Play Dates / Nanny Share

Menu / Bottles

Meal	Description / Time

Sleeps

Name: From: To:

☐ Check every 10 min

Expenses

Price	Description

Toileting / Nappies

Activities / Outings

SUNSCREEN ☐

Observations / Reflections

INITIAL

| MONDAY ☑ | TUESDAY ☐ | WEDNESDAY ☐ | THURSDAY ☐ | FRIDAY ☐ | SATURDAY ☐ | SUNDAY ☐ |

Our Day

DATE: START TIME: FINISH:

Family Communication to Nanny / Educator

Notes to Family / Supplies Needed

Play Dates / Nanny Share

Menu / Bottles

Meal	Description / Time

Sleeps

Name: From: To:

☐ Check every 10 min

Expenses

Price	Description

Toileting / Nappies

Activities / Outings

SUNSCREEN ☐

Observations / Reflections

INITIAL

© Butter Diaries

MONDAY	TUESDAY	WEDNESDAY	THURSDAY	FRIDAY	SATURDAY	SUNDAY
☑	☐	☐	☐	☐	☐	☐

Our Day

DATE: START TIME: FINISH:

Family Communication to Nanny / Educator

Notes to Family / Supplies Needed

Play Dates / Nanny Share

Menu / Bottles

Meal	Description / Time

Sleeps

Name: From: To:

☐ Check every 10 min

Expenses

Price	Description

Toileting / Nappies

Activities / Outings

☐ SUNSCREEN

Observations / Reflections

INITIAL

Our Day

| MONDAY ☑ | TUESDAY ☐ | WEDNESDAY ☐ | THURSDAY ☐ | FRIDAY ☐ | SATURDAY ☐ | SUNDAY ☐ |

DATE: START TIME: FINISH:

Family Communication to Nanny / Educator

Notes to Family / Supplies Needed

Play Dates / Nanny Share

Menu / Bottles

Meal	Description / Time

Sleeps

Name: From: To:

☐ Check every 10 min

Expenses

Price	Description

Toileting / Nappies

Activities / Outings

SUNSCREEN ☐

Observations / Reflections

INITIAL

| MONDAY ☑ | TUESDAY ☐ | WEDNESDAY ☐ | THURSDAY ☐ | FRIDAY ☐ | SATURDAY ☐ | SUNDAY ☐ |

Our Day

DATE: START TIME: FINISH:

Family Communication to Nanny / Educator

Notes to Family / Supplies Needed

Play Dates / Nanny Share

Menu / Bottles
Meal — Description / Time

Sleeps
Name: From: To:

☐ Check every 10 min

Expenses
Price — Description

Toileting / Nappies

Activities / Outings
☐ SUNSCREEN

Observations / Reflections

INITIAL

© Butler Diaries

| MONDAY ☑ | TUESDAY ☐ | WEDNESDAY ☐ | THURSDAY ☐ | FRIDAY ☐ | SATURDAY ☐ | SUNDAY ☐ |

Our Day

DATE: START TIME: FINISH:

Family Communication to Nanny / Educator

Notes to Family / Supplies Needed

Play Dates / Nanny Share

Menu / Bottles
Meal	Description / Time

Sleeps
Name: From: To:

☐ Check every 10 min

Expenses
Price	Description

Toileting / Nappies

Activities / Outings

SUNSCREEN ☐

Observations / Reflections

INITIAL

MONDAY	TUESDAY	WEDNESDAY	THURSDAY	FRIDAY	SATURDAY	SUNDAY
☑	☐	☐	☐	☐	☐	☐

Our Day

DATE: START TIME: FINISH:

Family Communication to Nanny / Educator

Notes to Family / Supplies Needed

Play Dates / Nanny Share

Menu / Bottles
Meal	Description / Time

Sleeps
Name: From: To:

☐ Check every 10 min

Expenses
Price	Description

Toileting / Nappies

Activities / Outings

SUNSCREEN ☐

Observations / Reflections

INITIAL

| MONDAY ☑ | TUESDAY ☐ | WEDNESDAY ☐ | THURSDAY ☐ | FRIDAY ☐ | SATURDAY ☐ | SUNDAY ☐ |

Our Day

DATE: START TIME: FINISH:

Family Communication to Nanny / Educator

Notes to Family / Supplies Needed

Play Dates / Nanny Share

Menu / Bottles

Meal	Description / Time

Sleeps

Name: From: To:

☐ Check every 10 min

Expenses

Price	Description

Toileting / Nappies

Activities / Outings

SUNSCREEN ☐

Observations / Reflections

INITIAL

© Butler Diaries

| MONDAY ☑ | TUESDAY ☐ | WEDNESDAY ☐ | THURSDAY ☐ | FRIDAY ☐ | SATURDAY ☐ | SUNDAY ☐ |

Our Day

DATE: START TIME: FINISH:

Family Communication to Nanny / Educator

Notes to Family / Supplies Needed

Play Dates / Nanny Share

Menu / Bottles

Meal	Description / Time

Sleeps

Name: From: To:

☐ Check every 10 min

Expenses

Price	Description

Toileting / Nappies

Activities / Outings

SUNSCREEN ☐

Observations / Reflections

INITIAL

Our Day

- [x] MONDAY
- [ ] TUESDAY
- [ ] WEDNESDAY
- [ ] THURSDAY
- [ ] FRIDAY
- [ ] SATURDAY
- [ ] SUNDAY

DATE: START TIME: FINISH:

Family Communication to Nanny / Educator

Notes to Family / Supplies Needed

Play Dates / Nanny Share

Menu / Bottles

Meal	Description / Time

Sleeps

Name: From: To:

- [ ] Check every 10 min

Expenses

Price	Description

Toileting / Nappies

Activities / Outings

- [ ] SUNSCREEN

Observations / Reflections

INITIAL

© Butler Diaries

Our Day

MONDAY	TUESDAY	WEDNESDAY	THURSDAY	FRIDAY	SATURDAY	SUNDAY
☑	☐	☐	☐	☐	☐	☐

DATE: START TIME: FINISH:

Family Communication to Nanny / Educator

Notes to Family / Supplies Needed

Play Dates / Nanny Share

Menu / Bottles
Meal	Description / Time

Sleeps
Name: From: To:

☐ Check every 10 min

Expenses
Price	Description

Toileting / Nappies

Activities / Outings

☐ SUNSCREEN

Observations / Reflections

INITIAL

© Butler Diaries

| MONDAY ☑ | TUESDAY ☐ | WEDNESDAY ☐ | THURSDAY ☐ | FRIDAY ☐ | SATURDAY ☐ | SUNDAY ☐ |

Our Day

DATE:　　　　　　　　START TIME:　　　　　　　FINISH:

Family Communication to Nanny / Educator

Notes to Family / Supplies Needed

Play Dates / Nanny Share

Menu / Bottles

Meal	Description / Time

Sleeps

Name:　　From:　　To:

☐ Check every 10 min

Expenses

Price	Description

Toileting / Nappies

Activities / Outings

SUNSCREEN ☐

Observations / Reflections

INITIAL

MONDAY	TUESDAY	WEDNESDAY	THURSDAY	FRIDAY	SATURDAY	SUNDAY
☑	☐	☐	☐	☐	☐	☐

Our Day

DATE: START TIME: FINISH:

Family Communication to Nanny / Educator

Notes to Family / Supplies Needed

Play Dates / Nanny Share

Menu / Bottles
Meal	Description / Time

Sleeps
Name: From: To:

☐ Check every 10 min

Expenses
Price	Description

Toileting / Nappies

Activities / Outings

SUNSCREEN ☐

Observations / Reflections

INITIAL

| MONDAY ☑ | TUESDAY ☐ | WEDNESDAY ☐ | THURSDAY ☐ | FRIDAY ☐ | SATURDAY ☐ | SUNDAY ☐ |

Our Day

DATE: START TIME: FINISH:

Family Communication to Nanny / Educator

Notes to Family / Supplies Needed

Play Dates / Nanny Share

Menu / Bottles
Meal	Description / Time

Sleeps
Name: From: To:

☐ Check every 10 min

Expenses
Price	Description

Toileting / Nappies

Activities / Outings

SUNSCREEN ☐

Observations / Reflections

INITIAL

MONDAY	TUESDAY	WEDNESDAY	THURSDAY	FRIDAY	SATURDAY	SUNDAY
☑	☐	☐	☐	☐	☐	☐

Our Day

DATE: START TIME: FINISH:

Family Communication to Nanny / Educator

Notes to Family / Supplies Needed

Play Dates / Nanny Share

Menu / Bottles

Meal	Description / Time

Sleeps

Name: From: To:

☐ Check every 10 min

Expenses

Price	Description

Toileting / Nappies

Activities / Outings

SUNSCREEN ☐

Observations / Reflections

INITIAL

© Butler Diaries

Our Day

| MONDAY ☑ | TUESDAY ☐ | WEDNESDAY ☐ | THURSDAY ☐ | FRIDAY ☐ | SATURDAY ☐ | SUNDAY ☐ |

DATE: START TIME: FINISH:

Family Communication to Nanny / Educator

Notes to Family / Supplies Needed

Play Dates / Nanny Share

Menu / Bottles

Meal	Description / Time

Sleeps

Name: From: To:

☐ Check every 10 min

Expenses

Price	Description

Toileting / Nappies

Activities / Outings

SUNSCREEN ☐

Observations / Reflections

INITIAL

© Butler Diaries

| MONDAY ☑ | TUESDAY ☐ | WEDNESDAY ☐ | THURSDAY ☐ | FRIDAY ☐ | SATURDAY ☐ | SUNDAY ☐ |

Our Day

DATE: START TIME: FINISH:

Family Communication to Nanny / Educator

Notes to Family / Supplies Needed

Play Dates / Nanny Share

Menu / Bottles
Meal	Description / Time

Sleeps
Name: From: To:

☐ Check every 10 min

Expenses
Price	Description

Toileting / Nappies

Activities / Outings

SUNSCREEN ☐

Observations / Reflections

INITIAL

© Butler Diaries

| MONDAY ☑ | TUESDAY ☐ | WEDNESDAY ☐ | THURSDAY ☐ | FRIDAY ☐ | SATURDAY ☐ | SUNDAY ☐ |

Our Day

DATE: START TIME: FINISH:

Family Communication to Nanny / Educator

Notes to Family / Supplies Needed

Play Dates / Nanny Share

Menu / Bottles

Meal	Description / Time

Sleeps

Name: From: To:

☐ Check every 10 min

Expenses

Price	Description

Toileting / Nappies

Activities / Outings

SUNSCREEN ☐

Observations / Reflections

INITIAL

© Butter Diaries

Our Day

MONDAY	TUESDAY	WEDNESDAY	THURSDAY	FRIDAY	SATURDAY	SUNDAY
☑	☐	☐	☐	☐	☐	☐

DATE: START TIME: FINISH:

Family Communication to Nanny / Educator

Notes to Family / Supplies Needed

Play Dates / Nanny Share

Menu / Bottles
Meal	Description / Time

Sleeps
Name: From: To:

☐ Check every 10 min

Expenses
Price	Description

Toileting / Nappies

Activities / Outings
☐ SUNSCREEN

Observations / Reflections

INITIAL

© Butler Diaries

Our Day

| MONDAY ☑ | TUESDAY ☐ | WEDNESDAY ☐ | THURSDAY ☐ | FRIDAY ☐ | SATURDAY ☐ | SUNDAY ☐ |

DATE: START TIME: FINISH:

Family Communication to Nanny / Educator

Notes to Family / Supplies Needed

Play Dates / Nanny Share

Menu / Bottles
Meal	Description / Time

Sleeps
Name: From: To:

☐ Check every 10 min

Expenses
Price	Description

Toileting / Nappies

Activities / Outings

SUNSCREEN ☐

Observations / Reflections

INITIAL

© Butler Diaries

| MONDAY ☑ | TUESDAY ☐ | WEDNESDAY ☐ | THURSDAY ☐ | FRIDAY ☐ | SATURDAY ☐ | SUNDAY ☐ |

Our Day

DATE: START TIME: FINISH:

Family Communication to Nanny / Educator

Notes to Family / Supplies Needed

Play Dates / Nanny Share

Menu / Bottles
Meal	Description / Time

Sleeps
Name: From: To:

☐ Check every 10 min

Expenses
Price	Description

Toileting / Nappies

Activities / Outings

SUNSCREEN ☐

Observations / Reflections

INITIAL

© Butler Diaries

| MONDAY ☑ | TUESDAY ☐ | WEDNESDAY ☐ | THURSDAY ☐ | FRIDAY ☐ | SATURDAY ☐ | SUNDAY ☐ |

Our Day

DATE: START TIME: FINISH:

Family Communication to Nanny / Educator

Notes to Family / Supplies Needed

Play Dates / Nanny Share

Menu / Bottles
Meal	Description / Time

Sleeps
Name: From: To:

☐ Check every 10 min

Expenses
Price	Description

Toileting / Nappies

Activities / Outings

SUNSCREEN ☐

Observations / Reflections

INITIAL

| MONDAY ☑ | TUESDAY ☐ | WEDNESDAY ☐ | THURSDAY ☐ | FRIDAY ☐ | SATURDAY ☐ | SUNDAY ☐ |

Our Day

DATE: START TIME: FINISH:

Family Communication to Nanny / Educator

Notes to Family / Supplies Needed

Play Dates / Nanny Share

Menu / Bottles
Meal	Description / Time

Sleeps
Name: From: To:

☐ Check every 10 min

Expenses
Price	Description

Toileting / Nappies

Activities / Outings

SUNSCREEN ☐

Observations / Reflections

INITIAL

© Butler Diaries

| MONDAY ☑ | TUESDAY ☐ | WEDNESDAY ☐ | THURSDAY ☐ | FRIDAY ☐ | SATURDAY ☐ | SUNDAY ☐ |

Our Day

DATE: START TIME: FINISH:

Family Communication to Nanny / Educator

Notes to Family / Supplies Needed

Play Dates / Nanny Share

Menu / Bottles

Meal	Description / Time

Sleeps

Name: From: To:

☐ Check every 10 min

Expenses

Price	Description

Toileting / Nappies

Activities / Outings

SUNSCREEN ☐

Observations / Reflections

INITIAL

© Butler Diaries

Our Day

| MONDAY ☑ | TUESDAY ☐ | WEDNESDAY ☐ | THURSDAY ☐ | FRIDAY ☐ | SATURDAY ☐ | SUNDAY ☐ |

DATE: START TIME: FINISH:

Family Communication to Nanny / Educator

Notes to Family / Supplies Needed

Play Dates / Nanny Share

Menu / Bottles

Meal	Description / Time

Sleeps

Name: From: To:

☐ Check every 10 min

Expenses

Price	Description

Toileting / Nappies

Activities / Outings

SUNSCREEN ☐

Observations / Reflections

INITIAL

Our Day

| MONDAY ☑ | TUESDAY ☐ | WEDNESDAY ☐ | THURSDAY ☐ | FRIDAY ☐ | SATURDAY ☐ | SUNDAY ☐ |

DATE: START TIME: FINISH:

Family Communication to Nanny / Educator

Notes to Family / Supplies Needed

Play Dates / Nanny Share

Menu / Bottles

Meal	Description / Time

Sleeps

Name: From: To:

☐ Check every 10 min

Expenses

Price	Description

Toileting / Nappies

Activities / Outings

SUNSCREEN ☐

Observations / Reflections

INITIAL

Our Day

| MONDAY ☑ | TUESDAY ☐ | WEDNESDAY ☐ | THURSDAY ☐ | FRIDAY ☐ | SATURDAY ☐ | SUNDAY ☐ |

DATE: START TIME: FINISH:

Family Communication to Nanny / Educator

Notes to Family / Supplies Needed

Play Dates / Nanny Share

Menu / Bottles

Meal	Description / Time

Sleeps

Name:	From:	To:

☐ Check every 10 min

Expenses

Price	Description

Toileting / Nappies

Activities / Outings

SUNSCREEN ☐

Observations / Reflections

INITIAL

MONDAY	TUESDAY	WEDNESDAY	THURSDAY	FRIDAY	SATURDAY	SUNDAY
☑	☐	☐	☐	☐	☐	☐

Our Day

DATE: START TIME: FINISH:

Family Communication to Nanny / Educator

Notes to Family / Supplies Needed

Play Dates / Nanny Share

Menu / Bottles

Meal	Description / Time

Sleeps

Name: From: To:

☐ Check every 10 min

Expenses

Price	Description

Toileting / Nappies

Activities / Outings

SUNSCREEN ☐

Observations / Reflections

INITIAL

© Butler Diaries

Our Day

| MONDAY ☑ | TUESDAY ☐ | WEDNESDAY ☐ | THURSDAY ☐ | FRIDAY ☐ | SATURDAY ☐ | SUNDAY ☐ |

DATE: START TIME: FINISH:

Family Communication to Nanny / Educator

Notes to Family / Supplies Needed

Play Dates / Nanny Share

Menu / Bottles

Meal	Description / Time

Sleeps

Name: From: To:

☐ Check every 10 min

Expenses

Price	Description

Toileting / Nappies

Activities / Outings

SUNSCREEN ☐

Observations / Reflections

INITIAL

| MONDAY ☑ | TUESDAY ☐ | WEDNESDAY ☐ | THURSDAY ☐ | FRIDAY ☐ | SATURDAY ☐ | SUNDAY ☐ |

Our Day

DATE: START TIME: FINISH:

Family Communication to Nanny / Educator

Notes to Family / Supplies Needed

Play Dates / Nanny Share

Menu / Bottles
Meal	Description / Time

Sleeps
Name: From: To:

☐ Check every 10 min

Expenses
Price	Description

Toileting / Nappies

Activities / Outings

SUNSCREEN ☐

Observations / Reflections

INITIAL

© Butler Diaries

MONDAY	TUESDAY	WEDNESDAY	THURSDAY	FRIDAY	SATURDAY	SUNDAY
☑	☐	☐	☐	☐	☐	☐

Our Day

DATE: START TIME: FINISH:

Family Communication to Nanny / Educator

Notes to Family / Supplies Needed

Play Dates / Nanny Share

Menu / Bottles

Meal	Description / Time

Sleeps

Name: From: To:

☐ Check every 10 min

Expenses

Price	Description

Toileting / Nappies

Activities / Outings

SUNSCREEN ☐

Observations / Reflections

INITIAL

© Butler Diaries

| MONDAY ☑ | TUESDAY ☐ | WEDNESDAY ☐ | THURSDAY ☐ | FRIDAY ☐ | SATURDAY ☐ | SUNDAY ☐ |

Our Day

DATE: START TIME: FINISH:

Family Communication to Nanny / Educator

Notes to Family / Supplies Needed

Play Dates / Nanny Share

Menu / Bottles
Meal	Description / Time

Sleeps
Name: From: To:

☐ Check every 10 min

Expenses
Price	Description

Toileting / Nappies

Activities / Outings

☐ SUNSCREEN

Observations / Reflections

INITIAL

Our Day

☑ MONDAY ☐ TUESDAY ☐ WEDNESDAY ☐ THURSDAY ☐ FRIDAY ☐ SATURDAY ☐ SUNDAY

DATE: START TIME: FINISH:

Family Communication to Nanny / Educator

Notes to Family / Supplies Needed

Play Dates / Nanny Share

Menu / Bottles

Meal	Description / Time

Sleeps

Name: From: To:

☐ Check every 10 min

Expenses

Price	Description

Toileting / Nappies

Activities / Outings

☐ SUNSCREEN

Observations / Reflections

INITIAL

© Butler Diaries

| MONDAY ☑ | TUESDAY ☐ | WEDNESDAY ☐ | THURSDAY ☐ | FRIDAY ☐ | SATURDAY ☐ | SUNDAY ☐ |

Our Day

DATE: START TIME: FINISH:

Family Communication to Nanny / Educator

Notes to Family / Supplies Needed

Play Dates / Nanny Share

Menu / Bottles
Meal	Description / Time

Sleeps
Name: From: To:

☐ Check every 10 min

Expenses
Price	Description

Toileting / Nappies

Activities / Outings

SUNSCREEN ☐

Observations / Reflections

INITIAL

MONDAY	TUESDAY	WEDNESDAY	THURSDAY	FRIDAY	SATURDAY	SUNDAY
☑	☐	☐	☐	☐	☐	☐

Our Day

DATE: START TIME: FINISH:

Family Communication to Nanny / Educator

Notes to Family / Supplies Needed

Play Dates / Nanny Share

Menu / Bottles

Meal	Description / Time

Sleeps

Name: From: To:

☐ Check every 10 min

Expenses

Price	Description

Toileting / Nappies

Activities / Outings

SUNSCREEN ☐

Observations / Reflections

INITIAL

| MONDAY ☑ | TUESDAY ☐ | WEDNESDAY ☐ | THURSDAY ☐ | FRIDAY ☐ | SATURDAY ☐ | SUNDAY ☐ |

Our Day

DATE: START TIME: FINISH:

Family Communication to Nanny / Educator

Notes to Family / Supplies Needed

Play Dates / Nanny Share

Menu / Bottles

Meal	Description / Time

Sleeps

Name: From: To:

☐ Check every 10 min

Expenses

Price	Description

Toileting / Nappies

Activities / Outings

☐ SUNSCREEN

Observations / Reflections

INITIAL

© Butler Diaries

Our Day

- [x] MONDAY
- [ ] TUESDAY
- [ ] WEDNESDAY
- [ ] THURSDAY
- [ ] FRIDAY
- [ ] SATURDAY
- [ ] SUNDAY

DATE: START TIME: FINISH:

Family Communication to Nanny / Educator

Notes to Family / Supplies Needed

Play Dates / Nanny Share

Menu / Bottles

Meal	Description / Time

Sleeps

Name: From: To:

- [ ] Check every 10 min

Expenses

Price	Description

Toileting / Nappies

Activities / Outings

SUNSCREEN [ ]

Observations / Reflections

INITIAL

| MONDAY ☑ | TUESDAY ☐ | WEDNESDAY ☐ | THURSDAY ☐ | FRIDAY ☐ | SATURDAY ☐ | SUNDAY ☐ |

Our Day

DATE: START TIME: FINISH:

Family Communication to Nanny / Educator

Notes to Family / Supplies Needed

Play Dates / Nanny Share

Menu / Bottles
Meal	Description / Time

Sleeps
Name: From: To:

☐ Check every 10 min

Expenses
Price	Description

Toileting / Nappies

Activities / Outings

SUNSCREEN ☐

Observations / Reflections

INITIAL

Our Day

MONDAY	TUESDAY	WEDNESDAY	THURSDAY	FRIDAY	SATURDAY	SUNDAY
☑ ☐	☐	☐	☐	☐	☐	☐

DATE: START TIME: FINISH:

Family Communication to Nanny / Educator

Notes to Family / Supplies Needed

Play Dates / Nanny Share

Menu / Bottles
Meal | Description / Time

Sleeps
Name: From: To:

☐ Check every 10 min

Expenses
Price | Description

Toileting / Nappies

Activities / Outings
SUNSCREEN ☐

Observations / Reflections

INITIAL

| MONDAY ☑ | TUESDAY ☐ | WEDNESDAY ☐ | THURSDAY ☐ | FRIDAY ☐ | SATURDAY ☐ | SUNDAY ☐ |

Our Day

DATE: START TIME: FINISH:

Family Communication to Nanny / Educator

Notes to Family / Supplies Needed

Play Dates / Nanny Share

Menu / Bottles
Meal	Description / Time

Sleeps
Name:	From:	To:

☐ Check every 10 min

Expenses
Price	Description

Toileting / Nappies

Activities / Outings

SUNSCREEN ☐

Observations / Reflections

INITIAL

© Butter Diaries

MONDAY	TUESDAY	WEDNESDAY	THURSDAY	FRIDAY	SATURDAY	SUNDAY
☑	☐	☐	☐	☐	☐	☐

Our Day

DATE: START TIME: FINISH:

Family Communication to Nanny / Educator

Notes to Family / Supplies Needed

Play Dates / Nanny Share

Menu / Bottles
Meal	Description / Time

Sleeps
Name: From: To:

☐ Check every 10 min

Expenses
Price	Description

Toileting / Nappies

Activities / Outings

SUNSCREEN ☐

Observations / Reflections

INITIAL

| MONDAY ☑ | TUESDAY ☐ | WEDNESDAY ☐ | THURSDAY ☐ | FRIDAY ☐ | SATURDAY ☐ | SUNDAY ☐ |

Our Day

DATE: START TIME: FINISH:

Family Communication to Nanny / Educator

Notes to Family / Supplies Needed

Play Dates / Nanny Share

Menu / Bottles

Meal	Description / Time

Sleeps

Name: From: To:

☐ Check every 10 min

Expenses

Price	Description

Toileting / Nappies

Activities / Outings

SUNSCREEN ☐

Observations / Reflections

INITIAL

© Butter Diaries

Our Day

| MONDAY ☑ | TUESDAY ☐ | WEDNESDAY ☐ | THURSDAY ☐ | FRIDAY ☐ | SATURDAY ☐ | SUNDAY ☐ |

DATE:　　　　　START TIME:　　　　　FINISH:

Family Communication to Nanny / Educator

Notes to Family / Supplies Needed

Play Dates / Nanny Share

Menu / Bottles
Meal　　Description / Time

Sleeps
Name:　From:　To:

☐ Check every 10 min

Expenses
Price　Description

Toileting / Nappies

Activities / Outings
☐ SUNSCREEN

Observations / Reflections

INITIAL

© Butler Diaries

| MONDAY ☑ | TUESDAY ☐ | WEDNESDAY ☐ | THURSDAY ☐ | FRIDAY ☐ | SATURDAY ☐ | SUNDAY ☐ |

Our Day

DATE: START TIME: FINISH:

Family Communication to Nanny / Educator

Notes to Family / Supplies Needed

Play Dates / Nanny Share

Menu / Bottles

Meal	Description / Time

Sleeps

Name: From: To:

☐ Check every 10 min

Expenses

Price	Description

Toileting / Nappies

Activities / Outings

SUNSCREEN ☐

Observations / Reflections

INITIAL

Our Day

| MONDAY ☑ | TUESDAY ☐ | WEDNESDAY ☐ | THURSDAY ☐ | FRIDAY ☐ | SATURDAY ☐ | SUNDAY ☐ |

DATE: START TIME: FINISH:

Family Communication to Nanny / Educator

Notes to Family / Supplies Needed

Play Dates / Nanny Share

Menu / Bottles
Meal	Description / Time

Sleeps
Name: From: To:

☐ Check every 10 min

Expenses
Price	Description

Toileting / Nappies

Activities / Outings

SUNSCREEN ☐

Observations / Reflections

INITIAL

Our Day

MONDAY ☑ TUESDAY ☐ WEDNESDAY ☐ THURSDAY ☐ FRIDAY ☐ SATURDAY ☐ SUNDAY ☐

DATE: START TIME: FINISH:

Family Communication to Nanny / Educator

Notes to Family / Supplies Needed

Play Dates / Nanny Share

Menu / Bottles

Meal	Description / Time

Sleeps

Name: From: To:

☐ Check every 10 min

Expenses

Price	Description

Toileting / Nappies

Activities / Outings

SUNSCREEN ☐

Observations / Reflections

INITIAL

Our Day

| MONDAY ☑ | TUESDAY ☐ | WEDNESDAY ☐ | THURSDAY ☐ | FRIDAY ☐ | SATURDAY ☐ | SUNDAY ☐ |

DATE: START TIME: FINISH:

Family Communication to Nanny / Educator

Notes to Family / Supplies Needed

Play Dates / Nanny Share

Menu / Bottles

Meal	Description / Time

Sleeps

Name: From: To:

☐ Check every 10 min

Expenses

Price	Description

Toileting / Nappies

Activities / Outings

☐ SUNSCREEN

Observations / Reflections

INITIAL

© Butler Diaries

Our Day

MONDAY ☑ TUESDAY ☐ WEDNESDAY ☐ THURSDAY ☐ FRIDAY ☐ SATURDAY ☐ SUNDAY ☐

DATE:　　　　　START TIME:　　　　　FINISH:

Family Communication to Nanny / Educator

Notes to Family / Supplies Needed

Play Dates / Nanny Share

Menu / Bottles
Meal	Description / Time

Sleeps
Name:　　From:　　To:

☐ Check every 10 min

Expenses
Price	Description

Toileting / Nappies

Activities / Outings

☐ SUNSCREEN

Observations / Reflections

INITIAL

© Butter Diaries

Our Day

| MONDAY ☑ | TUESDAY ☐ | WEDNESDAY ☐ | THURSDAY ☐ | FRIDAY ☐ | SATURDAY ☐ | SUNDAY ☐ |

DATE: START TIME: FINISH:

Family Communication to Nanny / Educator

Notes to Family / Supplies Needed

Play Dates / Nanny Share

Menu / Bottles
Meal	Description / Time

Sleeps
Name: From: To:

☐ Check every 10 min

Expenses
Price	Description

Toileting / Nappies

Activities / Outings

SUNSCREEN ☐

Observations / Reflections

INITIAL

© Butler Diaries

| MONDAY ☑ | TUESDAY ☐ | WEDNESDAY ☐ | THURSDAY ☐ | FRIDAY ☐ | SATURDAY ☐ | SUNDAY ☐ |

Our Day

DATE: START TIME: FINISH:

Family Communication to Nanny / Educator

Notes to Family / Supplies Needed

Play Dates / Nanny Share

Menu / Bottles
Meal	Description / Time

Sleeps
Name: From: To:

☐ Check every 10 min

Expenses
Price	Description

Toileting / Nappies

Activities / Outings

SUNSCREEN ☐

Observations / Reflections

INITIAL

Our Day

☑ MONDAY ☐ TUESDAY ☐ WEDNESDAY ☐ THURSDAY ☐ FRIDAY ☐ SATURDAY ☐ SUNDAY

DATE: START TIME: FINISH:

Family Communication to Nanny / Educator

Notes to Family / Supplies Needed

Play Dates / Nanny Share

Menu / Bottles

Meal	Description / Time

Sleeps

Name: From: To:

☐ Check every 10 min

Expenses

Price	Description

Toileting / Nappies

Activities / Outings

☐ SUNSCREEN

Observations / Reflections

INITIAL

Our Day

MONDAY ☑ TUESDAY ☐ WEDNESDAY ☐ THURSDAY ☐ FRIDAY ☐ SATURDAY ☐ SUNDAY ☐

DATE: START TIME: FINISH:

Family Communication to Nanny / Educator

Notes to Family / Supplies Needed

Play Dates / Nanny Share

Menu / Bottles

Meal	Description / Time

Sleeps

Name: From: To:

☐ Check every 10 min

Expenses

Price	Description

Toileting / Nappies

Activities / Outings

SUNSCREEN ☐

Observations / Reflections

INITIAL

| MONDAY ☑ | TUESDAY ☐ | WEDNESDAY ☐ | THURSDAY ☐ | FRIDAY ☐ | SATURDAY ☐ | SUNDAY ☐ |

Our Day

DATE: START TIME: FINISH:

Family Communication to Nanny / Educator

Notes to Family / Supplies Needed

Play Dates / Nanny Share

Menu / Bottles
Meal	Description / Time

Sleeps
Name: From: To:

☐ Check every 10 min

Expenses
Price	Description

Toileting / Nappies

Activities / Outings
SUNSCREEN ☐

Observations / Reflections

INITIAL

| MONDAY ☑ | TUESDAY ☐ | WEDNESDAY ☐ | THURSDAY ☐ | FRIDAY ☐ | SATURDAY ☐ | SUNDAY ☐ |

Our Day

DATE: START TIME: FINISH:

Family Communication to Nanny / Educator

Notes to Family / Supplies Needed

Play Dates / Nanny Share

Menu / Bottles

Meal	Description / Time

Sleeps

Name: From: To:

☐ Check every 10 min

Expenses

Price	Description

Toileting / Nappies

Activities / Outings

SUNSCREEN ☐

Observations / Reflections

INITIAL

© Butler Diaries

| MONDAY ☑ | TUESDAY ☐ | WEDNESDAY ☐ | THURSDAY ☐ | FRIDAY ☐ | SATURDAY ☐ | SUNDAY ☐ |

Our Day

DATE: START TIME: FINISH:

Family Communication to Nanny / Educator

Notes to Family / Supplies Needed

Play Dates / Nanny Share

Menu / Bottles
Meal	Description / Time

Sleeps
Name: From: To:

☐ Check every 10 min

Expenses
Price	Description

Toileting / Nappies

Activities / Outings

SUNSCREEN ☐

Observations / Reflections

INITIAL

| MONDAY ☑ | TUESDAY ☐ | WEDNESDAY ☐ | THURSDAY ☐ | FRIDAY ☐ | SATURDAY ☐ | SUNDAY ☐ |

Our Day

DATE: START TIME: FINISH:

Family Communication to Nanny / Educator

Notes to Family / Supplies Needed

Play Dates / Nanny Share

Menu / Bottles

Meal	Description / Time

Sleeps

Name: From: To:

☐ Check every 10 min

Expenses

Price	Description

Toileting / Nappies

Activities / Outings

SUNSCREEN ☐

Observations / Reflections

INITIAL

| MONDAY ☑ | TUESDAY ☐ | WEDNESDAY ☐ | THURSDAY ☐ | FRIDAY ☐ | SATURDAY ☐ | SUNDAY ☐ |

Our Day

DATE: START TIME: FINISH:

Family Communication to Nanny / Educator

Notes to Family / Supplies Needed

Play Dates / Nanny Share

Menu / Bottles
Meal	Description / Time

Sleeps
Name: From: To:

☐ Check every 10 min

Expenses
Price	Description

Toileting / Nappies

Activities / Outings

SUNSCREEN ☐

Observations / Reflections

INITIAL

| MONDAY ☑ | TUESDAY ☐ | WEDNESDAY ☐ | THURSDAY ☐ | FRIDAY ☐ | SATURDAY ☐ | SUNDAY ☐ |

Our Day

DATE:　　　　　START TIME:　　　　　FINISH:

Family Communication to Nanny / Educator

Notes to Family / Supplies Needed

Play Dates / Nanny Share

Menu / Bottles
Meal	Description / Time

Sleeps
Name:　　From:　　To:

☐ Check every 10 min

Expenses
Price	Description

Toileting / Nappies

Activities / Outings

SUNSCREEN ☐

Observations / Reflections

INITIAL

© Butler Diaries

| MONDAY ☑ | TUESDAY ☐ | WEDNESDAY ☐ | THURSDAY ☐ | FRIDAY ☐ | SATURDAY ☐ | SUNDAY ☐ |

Our Day

DATE: START TIME: FINISH:

Family Communication to Nanny / Educator

Notes to Family / Supplies Needed

Play Dates / Nanny Share

Menu / Bottles
Meal	Description / Time

Sleeps
Name: From: To:

☐ Check every 10 min

Expenses
Price	Description

Toileting / Nappies

Activities / Outings   SUNSCREEN ☐

Observations / Reflections

INITIAL

| MONDAY ☑ | TUESDAY ☐ | WEDNESDAY ☐ | THURSDAY ☐ | FRIDAY ☐ | SATURDAY ☐ | SUNDAY ☐ |

Our Day

DATE: START TIME: FINISH:

Family Communication to Nanny / Educator

Notes to Family / Supplies Needed

Play Dates / Nanny Share

Menu / Bottles

Meal	Description / Time

Sleeps

Name: From: To:

☐ Check every 10 min

Expenses

Price	Description

Toileting / Nappies

Activities / Outings

SUNSCREEN ☐

Observations / Reflections

INITIAL

© Butler Diaries

| MONDAY ☑ | TUESDAY ☐ | WEDNESDAY ☐ | THURSDAY ☐ | FRIDAY ☐ | SATURDAY ☐ | SUNDAY ☐ |

Our Day

DATE: START TIME: FINISH:

Family Communication to Nanny / Educator

Notes to Family / Supplies Needed

Play Dates / Nanny Share

Menu / Bottles

Meal	Description / Time

Sleeps

Name: From: To:

☐ Check every 10 min

Expenses

Price	Description

Toileting / Nappies

Activities / Outings

SUNSCREEN ☐

Observations / Reflections

INITIAL

| MONDAY ☑ | TUESDAY ☐ | WEDNESDAY ☐ | THURSDAY ☐ | FRIDAY ☐ | SATURDAY ☐ | SUNDAY ☐ |

Our Day

DATE: START TIME: FINISH:

Family Communication to Nanny / Educator

Notes to Family / Supplies Needed

Play Dates / Nanny Share

Menu / Bottles

Meal	Description / Time

Sleeps

Name: From: To:

☐ Check every 10 min

Expenses

Price	Description

Toileting / Nappies

Activities / Outings

SUNSCREEN ☐

Observations / Reflections

INITIAL

Our Day

| MONDAY ☑ | TUESDAY ☐ | WEDNESDAY ☐ | THURSDAY ☐ | FRIDAY ☐ | SATURDAY ☐ | SUNDAY ☐ |

DATE: START TIME: FINISH:

Family Communication to Nanny / Educator

Notes to Family / Supplies Needed

Play Dates / Nanny Share

Menu / Bottles
Meal	Description / Time

Sleeps
Name: From: To:

☐ Check every 10 min

Expenses
Price	Description

Toileting / Nappies

Activities / Outings
SUNSCREEN ☐

Observations / Reflections

INITIAL

© Butler Diaries

Our Day

| MONDAY ☑ | TUESDAY ☐ | WEDNESDAY ☐ | THURSDAY ☐ | FRIDAY ☐ | SATURDAY ☐ | SUNDAY ☐ |

DATE: START TIME: FINISH:

Family Communication to Nanny / Educator

Notes to Family / Supplies Needed

Play Dates / Nanny Share

Menu / Bottles
Meal	Description / Time

Sleeps
Name: From: To:

☐ Check every 10 min

Expenses
Price	Description

Toileting / Nappies

Activities / Outings

SUNSCREEN ☐

Observations / Reflections

INITIAL

| MONDAY ☑ | TUESDAY ☐ | WEDNESDAY ☐ | THURSDAY ☐ | FRIDAY ☐ | SATURDAY ☐ | SUNDAY ☐ |

Our Day

DATE: START TIME: FINISH:

Family Communication to Nanny / Educator

Notes to Family / Supplies Needed

Play Dates / Nanny Share

Menu / Bottles
Meal	Description / Time

Sleeps
Name: From: To:

☐ Check every 10 min

Expenses
Price	Description

Toileting / Nappies

Activities / Outings

SUNSCREEN ☐

Observations / Reflections

INITIAL

Our Day

| MONDAY ☑ | TUESDAY ☐ | WEDNESDAY ☐ | THURSDAY ☐ | FRIDAY ☐ | SATURDAY ☐ | SUNDAY ☐ |

DATE: START TIME: FINISH:

Family Communication to Nanny / Educator

Notes to Family / Supplies Needed

Play Dates / Nanny Share

Menu / Bottles

Meal	Description / Time

Sleeps

Name: From: To:

☐ Check every 10 min

Expenses

Price	Description

Toileting / Nappies

Activities / Outings

SUNSCREEN ☐

Observations / Reflections

INITIAL

| MONDAY ☑ | TUESDAY ☐ | WEDNESDAY ☐ | THURSDAY ☐ | FRIDAY ☐ | SATURDAY ☐ | SUNDAY ☐ |

Our Day

DATE: START TIME: FINISH:

Family Communication to Nanny / Educator

Notes to Family / Supplies Needed

Play Dates / Nanny Share

Menu / Bottles

Meal	Description / Time

Sleeps

Name: From: To:

☐ Check every 10 min

Expenses

Price	Description

Toileting / Nappies

Activities / Outings

SUNSCREEN ☐

Observations / Reflections

INITIAL

© Butler Diaries

Our Day

| MONDAY ☑ | TUESDAY ☐ | WEDNESDAY ☐ | THURSDAY ☐ | FRIDAY ☐ | SATURDAY ☐ | SUNDAY ☐ |

DATE: START TIME: FINISH:

Family Communication to Nanny / Educator

Notes to Family / Supplies Needed

Play Dates / Nanny Share

Menu / Bottles

Meal	Description / Time

Sleeps

Name: From: To:

☐ Check every 10 min

Expenses

Price	Description

Toileting / Nappies

Activities / Outings

SUNSCREEN ☐

Observations / Reflections

INITIAL

© Butler Diaries

| MONDAY ☑ | TUESDAY ☐ | WEDNESDAY ☐ | THURSDAY ☐ | FRIDAY ☐ | SATURDAY ☐ | SUNDAY ☐ |

Our Day

DATE: START TIME: FINISH:

Family Communication to Nanny / Educator

Notes to Family / Supplies Needed

Play Dates / Nanny Share

Menu / Bottles

Meal	Description / Time

Sleeps

Name: From: To:

☐ Check every 10 min

Expenses

Price	Description

Toileting / Nappies

Activities / Outings

SUNSCREEN ☐

Observations / Reflections

INITIAL

© Butler Diaries

| MONDAY ☑ | TUESDAY ☐ | WEDNESDAY ☐ | THURSDAY ☐ | FRIDAY ☐ | SATURDAY ☐ | SUNDAY ☐ |

Our Day

DATE: START TIME: FINISH:

Family Communication to Nanny / Educator

Notes to Family / Supplies Needed

Play Dates / Nanny Share

Menu / Bottles

Meal	Description / Time

Sleeps

Name: From: To:

☐ Check every 10 min

Expenses

Price	Description

Toileting / Nappies

Activities / Outings

SUNSCREEN ☐

Observations / Reflections

INITIAL

| MONDAY ☑ | TUESDAY ☐ | WEDNESDAY ☐ | THURSDAY ☐ | FRIDAY ☐ | SATURDAY ☐ | SUNDAY ☐ |

Our Day

DATE: _____ START TIME: _____ FINISH: _____

Family Communication to Nanny / Educator

Notes to Family / Supplies Needed

Play Dates / Nanny Share

Menu / Bottles

Meal	Description / Time

Sleeps

Name: From: To:

☐ Check every 10 min

Expenses

Price	Description

Toileting / Nappies

Activities / Outings

SUNSCREEN ☐

Observations / Reflections

INITIAL

© Butler Diaries

MONDAY	TUESDAY	WEDNESDAY	THURSDAY	FRIDAY	SATURDAY	SUNDAY
☑	☐	☐	☐	☐	☐	☐

Our Day

DATE: START TIME: FINISH:

Family Communication to Nanny / Educator

Notes to Family / Supplies Needed

Play Dates / Nanny Share

Menu / Bottles
Meal	Description / Time

Sleeps
Name: From: To:

☐ Check every 10 min

Expenses
Price	Description

Toileting / Nappies

Activities / Outings   SUNSCREEN ☐

Observations / Reflections

INITIAL

Our Day

- [x] MONDAY
- [ ] TUESDAY
- [ ] WEDNESDAY
- [ ] THURSDAY
- [ ] FRIDAY
- [ ] SATURDAY
- [ ] SUNDAY

DATE: START TIME: FINISH:

Family Communication to Nanny / Educator

Notes to Family / Supplies Needed

Play Dates / Nanny Share

Menu / Bottles

Meal	Description / Time

Sleeps

Name: From: To:

- [ ] Check every 10 min

Expenses

Price	Description

Toileting / Nappies

Activities / Outings

SUNSCREEN [ ]

Observations / Reflections

INITIAL

© Butler Diaries

| MONDAY ☑ | TUESDAY ☐ | WEDNESDAY ☐ | THURSDAY ☐ | FRIDAY ☐ | SATURDAY ☐ | SUNDAY ☐ |

Our Day

DATE: START TIME: FINISH:

Family Communication to Nanny / Educator

Notes to Family / Supplies Needed

Play Dates / Nanny Share

Menu / Bottles
Meal	Description / Time

Sleeps
Name: From: To:

☐ Check every 10 min

Expenses
Price	Description

Toileting / Nappies

Activities / Outings
SUNSCREEN ☐

Observations / Reflections

INITIAL

© Butter Diaries

MONDAY	TUESDAY	WEDNESDAY	THURSDAY	FRIDAY	SATURDAY	SUNDAY
☑	☐	☐	☐	☐	☐	☐

DATE:　　　　　START TIME:　　　　　FINISH:

Our Day

Family Communication to Nanny / Educator

Notes to Family / Supplies Needed

Play Dates / Nanny Share

Menu / Bottles

Meal	Description / Time

Sleeps

Name:　　From:　　To:

☐ Check every 10 min

Expenses

Price	Description

Toileting / Nappies

Activities / Outings

☐ SUNSCREEN

Observations / Reflections

INITIAL

© Butler Diaries

| MONDAY ☑ | TUESDAY ☐ | WEDNESDAY ☐ | THURSDAY ☐ | FRIDAY ☐ | SATURDAY ☐ | SUNDAY ☐ |

Our Day

DATE: START TIME: FINISH:

Family Communication to Nanny / Educator

Notes to Family / Supplies Needed

Play Dates / Nanny Share

Menu / Bottles

Meal	Description / Time

Sleeps

Name: From: To:

☐ Check every 10 min

Expenses

Price	Description

Toileting / Nappies

Activities / Outings

SUNSCREEN ☐

Observations / Reflections

INITIAL

© Butler Diaries

| MONDAY ☑ | TUESDAY ☐ | WEDNESDAY ☐ | THURSDAY ☐ | FRIDAY ☐ | SATURDAY ☐ | SUNDAY ☐ |

Our Day

DATE:　　　　　　　START TIME: 　　　　　　　FINISH:

Family Communication to Nanny / Educator

Notes to Family / Supplies Needed

Play Dates / Nanny Share

Menu / Bottles
Meal | Description / Time

Sleeps
Name:　　From:　　To:

☐ Check every 10 min

Expenses
Price | Description

Toileting / Nappies

Activities / Outings

SUNSCREEN ☐

Observations / Reflections

INITIAL

Our Day

| MONDAY ☑ | TUESDAY ☐ | WEDNESDAY ☐ | THURSDAY ☐ | FRIDAY ☐ | SATURDAY ☐ | SUNDAY ☐ |

DATE: START TIME: FINISH:

Family Communication to Nanny / Educator

Notes to Family / Supplies Needed

Play Dates / Nanny Share

Menu / Bottles

Meal	Description / Time

Sleeps

Name: From: To:

☐ Check every 10 min

Expenses

Price	Description

Toileting / Nappies

Activities / Outings

SUNSCREEN ☐

Observations / Reflections

INITIAL

© Butler Diaries

MONDAY	TUESDAY	WEDNESDAY	THURSDAY	FRIDAY	SATURDAY	SUNDAY
☑	☐	☐	☐	☐	☐	☐

Our Day

DATE: START TIME: FINISH:

Family Communication to Nanny / Educator

Notes to Family / Supplies Needed

Play Dates / Nanny Share

Menu / Bottles

Meal	Description / Time

Sleeps

Name: From: To:

☐ Check every 10 min

Expenses

Price	Description

Toileting / Nappies

Activities / Outings

☐ SUNSCREEN

Observations / Reflections

INITIAL

© Butler Diaries

| MONDAY ☑ | TUESDAY ☐ | WEDNESDAY ☐ | THURSDAY ☐ | FRIDAY ☐ | SATURDAY ☐ | SUNDAY ☐ |

Our Day

DATE: START TIME: FINISH:

Family Communication to Nanny / Educator

Notes to Family / Supplies Needed

Play Dates / Nanny Share

Menu / Bottles

Meal	Description / Time

Sleeps

Name: From: To:

☐ Check every 10 min

Expenses

Price	Description

Toileting / Nappies

Activities / Outings

SUNSCREEN ☐

Observations / Reflections

INITIAL

© Butler Diaries

| MONDAY ☑ | TUESDAY ☐ | WEDNESDAY ☐ | THURSDAY ☐ | FRIDAY ☐ | SATURDAY ☐ | SUNDAY ☐ |

Our Day

DATE: START TIME: FINISH:

Family Communication to Nanny / Educator

Notes to Family / Supplies Needed

Play Dates / Nanny Share

Menu / Bottles
Meal	Description / Time

Sleeps
Name: From: To:

☐ Check every 10 min

Expenses
Price	Description

Toileting / Nappies

Activities / Outings

SUNSCREEN ☐

Observations / Reflections

INITIAL

Our Day

MONDAY ☑ TUESDAY ☐ WEDNESDAY ☐ THURSDAY ☐ FRIDAY ☐ SATURDAY ☐ SUNDAY ☐

DATE: START TIME: FINISH:

Family Communication to Nanny / Educator

Notes to Family / Supplies Needed

Play Dates / Nanny Share

Menu / Bottles

Meal	Description / Time

Sleeps

Name: From: To:

☐ Check every 10 min

Expenses

Price	Description

Toileting / Nappies

Activities / Outings

SUNSCREEN ☐

Observations / Reflections

INITIAL

Our Day

MONDAY ☑ TUESDAY ☐ WEDNESDAY ☐ THURSDAY ☐ FRIDAY ☐ SATURDAY ☐ SUNDAY ☐

DATE: START TIME: FINISH:

Family Communication to Nanny / Educator

Notes to Family / Supplies Needed

Play Dates / Nanny Share

Menu / Bottles

Meal	Description / Time

Sleeps

Name: From: To:

☐ Check every 10 min

Expenses

Price	Description

Toileting / Nappies

Activities / Outings

☐ SUNSCREEN

Observations / Reflections

INITIAL

© Butler Diaries

| MONDAY ☑ | TUESDAY ☐ | WEDNESDAY ☐ | THURSDAY ☐ | FRIDAY ☐ | SATURDAY ☐ | SUNDAY ☐ |

Our Day

DATE: START TIME: FINISH:

Family Communication to Nanny / Educator

Notes to Family / Supplies Needed

Play Dates / Nanny Share

Menu / Bottles
Meal	Description / Time

Sleeps
Name: From: To:

☐ Check every 10 min

Expenses
Price	Description

Toileting / Nappies

Activities / Outings

SUNSCREEN ☐

Observations / Reflections

INITIAL

© Butler Diaries

| MONDAY ☑ | TUESDAY ☐ | WEDNESDAY ☐ | THURSDAY ☐ | FRIDAY ☐ | SATURDAY ☐ | SUNDAY ☐ |

Our Day

DATE: START TIME: FINISH:

Family Communication to Nanny / Educator

Notes to Family / Supplies Needed

Play Dates / Nanny Share

Menu / Bottles
Meal	Description / Time

Sleeps
Name: From: To:

☐ Check every 10 min

Expenses
Price	Description

Toileting / Nappies

Activities / Outings

SUNSCREEN ☐

Observations / Reflections

INITIAL

© Butler Diaries

Our Day

| MONDAY ☑ | TUESDAY ☐ | WEDNESDAY ☐ | THURSDAY ☐ | FRIDAY ☐ | SATURDAY ☐ | SUNDAY ☐ |

DATE: START TIME: FINISH:

Family Communication to Nanny / Educator

Notes to Family / Supplies Needed

Play Dates / Nanny Share

Menu / Bottles

Meal	Description / Time

Sleeps

Name: From: To:

☐ Check every 10 min

Expenses

Price	Description

Toileting / Nappies

Activities / Outings

SUNSCREEN ☐

Observations / Reflections

INITIAL

| MONDAY ☑ | TUESDAY ☐ | WEDNESDAY ☐ | THURSDAY ☐ | FRIDAY ☐ | SATURDAY ☐ | SUNDAY ☐ |

Our Day

DATE: START TIME: FINISH:

Family Communication to Nanny / Educator

Notes to Family / Supplies Needed

Play Dates / Nanny Share

Menu / Bottles

Meal	Description / Time

Sleeps

Name:	From:	To:

☐ Check every 10 min

Expenses

Price	Description

Toileting / Nappies

Activities / Outings

SUNSCREEN ☐

Observations / Reflections

INITIAL

© Butler Diaries

MONDAY	TUESDAY	WEDNESDAY	THURSDAY	FRIDAY	SATURDAY	SUNDAY
☑	☐	☐	☐	☐	☐	☐

Our Day

DATE: START TIME: FINISH:

Family Communication to Nanny / Educator

Notes to Family / Supplies Needed

Play Dates / Nanny Share

Menu / Bottles
Meal	Description / Time

Sleeps
Name: From: To:

☐ Check every 10 min

Expenses
Price	Description

Toileting / Nappies

Activities / Outings
SUNSCREEN ☐

Observations / Reflections

INITIAL

© Butler Diaries

| MONDAY ☑ | TUESDAY ☐ | WEDNESDAY ☐ | THURSDAY ☐ | FRIDAY ☐ | SATURDAY ☐ | SUNDAY ☐ |

Our Day

DATE: START TIME: FINISH:

Family Communication to Nanny / Educator

Notes to Family / Supplies Needed

Play Dates / Nanny Share

Menu / Bottles

Meal	Description / Time

Sleeps

Name: From: To:

☐ Check every 10 min

Expenses

Price	Description

Toileting / Nappies

Activities / Outings

SUNSCREEN ☐

Observations / Reflections

INITIAL

Our Day

| MONDAY ☑ | TUESDAY ☐ | WEDNESDAY ☐ | THURSDAY ☐ | FRIDAY ☐ | SATURDAY ☐ | SUNDAY ☐ |

DATE: START TIME: FINISH:

Family Communication to Nanny / Educator

Notes to Family / Supplies Needed

Play Dates / Nanny Share

Menu / Bottles
Meal	Description / Time

Sleeps
Name: From: To:

☐ Check every 10 min

Expenses
Price	Description

Toileting / Nappies

Activities / Outings

SUNSCREEN ☐

Observations / Reflections

INITIAL

| MONDAY ☑ | TUESDAY ☐ | WEDNESDAY ☐ | THURSDAY ☐ | FRIDAY ☐ | SATURDAY ☐ | SUNDAY ☐ |

Our Day

DATE: START TIME: FINISH:

Family Communication to Nanny / Educator

Notes to Family / Supplies Needed

Play Dates / Nanny Share

Menu / Bottles

Meal	Description / Time

Sleeps

Name: From: To:

☐ Check every 10 min

Expenses

Price	Description

Toileting / Nappies

Activities / Outings

SUNSCREEN ☐

Observations / Reflections

INITIAL

© Butler Diaries

| MONDAY ☑ | TUESDAY ☐ | WEDNESDAY ☐ | THURSDAY ☐ | FRIDAY ☐ | SATURDAY ☐ | SUNDAY ☐ |

Our Day

DATE: START TIME: FINISH:

Family Communication to Nanny / Educator

Notes to Family / Supplies Needed

Play Dates / Nanny Share

Menu / Bottles

Meal	Description / Time

Sleeps

Name: From: To:

☐ Check every 10 min

Expenses

Price	Description

Toileting / Nappies

Activities / Outings

SUNSCREEN ☐

Observations / Reflections

INITIAL

| MONDAY ☑ | TUESDAY ☐ | WEDNESDAY ☐ | THURSDAY ☐ | FRIDAY ☐ | SATURDAY ☐ | SUNDAY ☐ |

Our Day

DATE: START TIME: FINISH:

Family Communication to Nanny / Educator

Notes to Family / Supplies Needed

Play Dates / Nanny Share

Menu / Bottles
Meal | Description / Time

Sleeps
Name: From: To:

☐ Check every 10 min

Expenses
Price | Description

Toileting / Nappies

Activities / Outings
SUNSCREEN ☐

Observations / Reflections

INITIAL

© Butler Diaries

| MONDAY ☑ | TUESDAY ☐ | WEDNESDAY ☐ | THURSDAY ☐ | FRIDAY ☐ | SATURDAY ☐ | SUNDAY ☐ |

Our Day

DATE: START TIME: FINISH:

Family Communication to Nanny / Educator

Notes to Family / Supplies Needed

Play Dates / Nanny Share

Menu / Bottles

Meal	Description / Time

Sleeps

Name: From: To:

☐ Check every 10 min

Expenses

Price	Description

Toileting / Nappies

Activities / Outings

SUNSCREEN ☐

Observations / Reflections

INITIAL

| MONDAY ☑ | TUESDAY ☐ | WEDNESDAY ☐ | THURSDAY ☐ | FRIDAY ☐ | SATURDAY ☐ | SUNDAY ☐ |

Our Day

DATE: START TIME: FINISH:

Family Communication to Nanny / Educator

Notes to Family / Supplies Needed

Play Dates / Nanny Share

Menu / Bottles

Meal	Description / Time

Sleeps

Name:	From:	To:

☐ Check every 10 min

Expenses

Price	Description

Toileting / Nappies

Activities / Outings

SUNSCREEN ☐

Observations / Reflections

INITIAL

© Butler Diaries

Our Day

- [x] MONDAY
- [ ] TUESDAY
- [ ] WEDNESDAY
- [ ] THURSDAY
- [ ] FRIDAY
- [ ] SATURDAY
- [ ] SUNDAY

DATE: START TIME: FINISH:

Family Communication to Nanny / Educator

Notes to Family / Supplies Needed

Play Dates / Nanny Share

Menu / Bottles

Meal	Description / Time

Sleeps

Name: From: To:

- [ ] Check every 10 min

Expenses

Price	Description

Toileting / Nappies

Activities / Outings

SUNSCREEN [ ]

Observations / Reflections

INITIAL

| MONDAY ☑ | TUESDAY ☐ | WEDNESDAY ☐ | THURSDAY ☐ | FRIDAY ☐ | SATURDAY ☐ | SUNDAY ☐ |

Our Day

DATE: START TIME: FINISH:

Family Communication to Nanny / Educator

Notes to Family / Supplies Needed

Play Dates / Nanny Share

Menu / Bottles
Meal	Description / Time

Sleeps
Name: From: To:

☐ Check every 10 min

Expenses
Price	Description

Toileting / Nappies

Activities / Outings
SUNSCREEN ☐

Observations / Reflections

INITIAL

© Butler Diaries

| MONDAY ☑ | TUESDAY ☐ | WEDNESDAY ☐ | THURSDAY ☐ | FRIDAY ☐ | SATURDAY ☐ | SUNDAY ☐ |

Our Day

DATE: START TIME: FINISH:

Family Communication to Nanny / Educator

Notes to Family / Supplies Needed

Play Dates / Nanny Share

Menu / Bottles
Meal	Description / Time

Sleeps
Name: From: To:

☐ Check every 10 min

Expenses
Price	Description

Toileting / Nappies

Activities / Outings
SUNSCREEN ☐

Observations / Reflections

INITIAL

MONDAY	TUESDAY	WEDNESDAY	THURSDAY	FRIDAY	SATURDAY	SUNDAY
☑ ☐	☐	☐	☐	☐	☐	☐

Our Day

DATE: START TIME: FINISH:

Family Communication to Nanny / Educator

Notes to Family / Supplies Needed

Play Dates / Nanny Share

Menu / Bottles
Meal	Description / Time

Sleeps
Name: From: To:

☐ Check every 10 min

Expenses
Price	Description

Toileting / Nappies

Activities / Outings

SUNSCREEN ☐

Observations / Reflections

INITIAL

© Butler Diaries

Our Day

☑ MONDAY ☐ TUESDAY ☐ WEDNESDAY ☐ THURSDAY ☐ FRIDAY ☐ SATURDAY ☐ SUNDAY

DATE: START TIME: FINISH:

Family Communication to Nanny / Educator

Notes to Family / Supplies Needed

Play Dates / Nanny Share

Menu / Bottles

Meal	Description / Time

Sleeps

Name: From: To:

☐ Check every 10 min

Expenses

Price	Description

Toileting / Nappies

Activities / Outings

SUNSCREEN ☐

Observations / Reflections

INITIAL

© Butler Diaries

| MONDAY ☑ | TUESDAY ☐ | WEDNESDAY ☐ | THURSDAY ☐ | FRIDAY ☐ | SATURDAY ☐ | SUNDAY ☐ |

Our Day

DATE: START TIME: FINISH:

Family Communication to Nanny / Educator

Notes to Family / Supplies Needed

Play Dates / Nanny Share

Menu / Bottles
Meal	Description / Time

Sleeps
Name: From: To:

☐ Check every 10 min

Expenses
Price	Description

Toileting / Nappies

Activities / Outings

SUNSCREEN ☐

Observations / Reflections

INITIAL

© Butler Diaries

Our Day

- [x] MONDAY
- [ ] TUESDAY
- [ ] WEDNESDAY
- [ ] THURSDAY
- [ ] FRIDAY
- [ ] SATURDAY
- [ ] SUNDAY

DATE: START TIME: FINISH:

Family Communication to Nanny / Educator

Notes to Family / Supplies Needed

Play Dates / Nanny Share

Menu / Bottles

Meal	Description / Time

Sleeps

Name:	From:	To:

- [ ] Check every 10 min

Expenses

Price	Description

Toileting / Nappies

Activities / Outings

SUNSCREEN [ ]

Observations / Reflections

INITIAL

MONDAY	TUESDAY	WEDNESDAY	THURSDAY	FRIDAY	SATURDAY	SUNDAY
☑	☐	☐	☐	☐	☐	☐

Our Day

DATE: START TIME: FINISH:

Family Communication to Nanny / Educator

Notes to Family / Supplies Needed

Play Dates / Nanny Share

Menu / Bottles

Meal	Description / Time

Sleeps

Name: From: To:

☐ Check every 10 min

Expenses

Price	Description

Toileting / Nappies

Activities / Outings

☐ SUNSCREEN

Observations / Reflections

INITIAL

© Butler Diaries

| MONDAY ☑ | TUESDAY ☐ | WEDNESDAY ☐ | THURSDAY ☐ | FRIDAY ☐ | SATURDAY ☐ | SUNDAY ☐ |

Our Day

DATE: START TIME: FINISH:

Family Communication to Nanny / Educator

Notes to Family / Supplies Needed

Play Dates / Nanny Share

Menu / Bottles

Meal	Description / Time

Sleeps

Name: From: To:

☐ Check every 10 min

Expenses

Price	Description

Toileting / Nappies

Activities / Outings

SUNSCREEN ☐

Observations / Reflections

INITIAL

Our Day

| MONDAY ☑ | TUESDAY ☐ | WEDNESDAY ☐ | THURSDAY ☐ | FRIDAY ☐ | SATURDAY ☐ | SUNDAY ☐ |

DATE: START TIME: FINISH:

Family Communication to Nanny / Educator

Notes to Family / Supplies Needed

Play Dates / Nanny Share

Menu / Bottles

Meal	Description / Time

Sleeps

Name: From: To:

☐ Check every 10 min

Expenses

Price	Description

Toileting / Nappies

Activities / Outings

SUNSCREEN ☐

Observations / Reflections

INITIAL

© Butler Diaries

| MONDAY ☑ | TUESDAY ☐ | WEDNESDAY ☐ | THURSDAY ☐ | FRIDAY ☐ | SATURDAY ☐ | SUNDAY ☐ |

Our Day

DATE: START TIME: FINISH:

Family Communication to Nanny / Educator

Notes to Family / Supplies Needed

Play Dates / Nanny Share

Menu / Bottles

Meal	Description / Time

Sleeps

Name:	From:	To:

☐ Check every 10 min

Expenses

Price	Description

Toileting / Nappies

Activities / Outings

SUNSCREEN ☐

Observations / Reflections

INITIAL

© Butter Diaries

| MONDAY ☑ | TUESDAY ☐ | WEDNESDAY ☐ | THURSDAY ☐ | FRIDAY ☐ | SATURDAY ☐ | SUNDAY ☐ |

Our Day

DATE: START TIME: FINISH:

Family Communication to Nanny / Educator

Notes to Family / Supplies Needed

Play Dates / Nanny Share

Menu / Bottles
Meal	Description / Time

Sleeps
Name: From: To:

☐ Check every 10 min

Expenses
Price	Description

Toileting / Nappies

Activities / Outings
SUNSCREEN ☐

Observations / Reflections

INITIAL

© Butler Diaries

Our Day

- [x] MONDAY
- [ ] TUESDAY
- [ ] WEDNESDAY
- [ ] THURSDAY
- [ ] FRIDAY
- [ ] SATURDAY
- [ ] SUNDAY

DATE: START TIME: FINISH:

Family Communication to Nanny / Educator

Notes to Family / Supplies Needed

Play Dates / Nanny Share

Menu / Bottles

Meal	Description / Time

Sleeps

Name: From: To:

- [ ] Check every 10 min

Expenses

Price	Description

Toileting / Nappies

Activities / Outings

SUNSCREEN
- [ ]

Observations / Reflections

INITIAL

| MONDAY ☑ | TUESDAY ☐ | WEDNESDAY ☐ | THURSDAY ☐ | FRIDAY ☐ | SATURDAY ☐ | SUNDAY ☐ |

Our Day

DATE: START TIME: FINISH:

Family Communication to Nanny / Educator

Notes to Family / Supplies Needed

Play Dates / Nanny Share

Menu / Bottles

Meal	Description / Time

Sleeps

Name: From: To:

☐ Check every 10 min

Expenses

Price	Description

Toileting / Nappies

Activities / Outings

SUNSCREEN ☐

Observations / Reflections

INITIAL

© Butler Diaries

Our Day

| MONDAY ☑ | TUESDAY ☐ | WEDNESDAY ☐ | THURSDAY ☐ | FRIDAY ☐ | SATURDAY ☐ | SUNDAY ☐ |

DATE: START TIME: FINISH:

Family Communication to Nanny / Educator

Notes to Family / Supplies Needed

Play Dates / Nanny Share

Menu / Bottles

Meal	Description / Time

Sleeps

Name: From: To:

☐ Check every 10 min

Expenses

Price	Description

Toileting / Nappies

Activities / Outings

SUNSCREEN ☐

Observations / Reflections

INITIAL

© Butler Diaries

Our Day

MONDAY	TUESDAY	WEDNESDAY	THURSDAY	FRIDAY	SATURDAY	SUNDAY
☑	☐	☐	☐	☐	☐	☐

DATE: START TIME: FINISH:

Family Communication to Nanny / Educator

Notes to Family / Supplies Needed

Play Dates / Nanny Share

Menu / Bottles
Meal	Description / Time

Sleeps
Name: From: To:

☐ Check every 10 min

Expenses
Price	Description

Toileting / Nappies

Activities / Outings

☐ SUNSCREEN

Observations / Reflections

INITIAL

© Butler Diaries

| MONDAY ☑ | TUESDAY ☐ | WEDNESDAY ☐ | THURSDAY ☐ | FRIDAY ☐ | SATURDAY ☐ | SUNDAY ☐ |

Our Day

DATE: START TIME: FINISH:

Family Communication to Nanny / Educator

Notes to Family / Supplies Needed

Play Dates / Nanny Share

Menu / Bottles

Meal	Description / Time

Sleeps

Name: From: To:

☐ Check every 10 min

Expenses

Price	Description

Toileting / Nappies

Activities / Outings

SUNSCREEN ☐

Observations / Reflections

INITIAL

© Butter Diaries

| MONDAY ☑ | TUESDAY ☐ | WEDNESDAY ☐ | THURSDAY ☐ | FRIDAY ☐ | SATURDAY ☐ | SUNDAY ☐ |

Our Day

DATE: START TIME: FINISH:

Family Communication to Nanny / Educator

Notes to Family / Supplies Needed

Play Dates / Nanny Share

Menu / Bottles

Meal	Description / Time

Sleeps

Name: From: To:

☐ Check every 10 min

Expenses

Price	Description

Toileting / Nappies

Activities / Outings

SUNSCREEN ☐

Observations / Reflections

INITIAL

© Butler Diaries

| MONDAY ☑ | TUESDAY ☐ | WEDNESDAY ☐ | THURSDAY ☐ | FRIDAY ☐ | SATURDAY ☐ | SUNDAY ☐ |

Our Day

DATE: START TIME: FINISH:

Family Communication to Nanny / Educator

Notes to Family / Supplies Needed

Play Dates / Nanny Share

Menu / Bottles

Meal	Description / Time

Sleeps

Name: From: To:

☐ Check every 10 min

Expenses

Price	Description

Toileting / Nappies

Activities / Outings

SUNSCREEN ☐

Observations / Reflections

INITIAL

© Butler Diaries

| MONDAY ☑ | TUESDAY ☐ | WEDNESDAY ☐ | THURSDAY ☐ | FRIDAY ☐ | SATURDAY ☐ | SUNDAY ☐ |

Our Day

DATE: START TIME: FINISH:

Family Communication to Nanny / Educator

Notes to Family / Supplies Needed

Play Dates / Nanny Share

Menu / Bottles
Meal	Description / Time

Sleeps
Name: From: To:

☐ Check every 10 min

Expenses
Price	Description

Toileting / Nappies

Activities / Outings

☐ SUNSCREEN

Observations / Reflections

INITIAL

© Butler Diaries

| MONDAY ☑ | TUESDAY ☐ | WEDNESDAY ☐ | THURSDAY ☐ | FRIDAY ☐ | SATURDAY ☐ | SUNDAY ☐ |

Our Day

DATE: START TIME: FINISH:

Family Communication to Nanny / Educator

Notes to Family / Supplies Needed

Play Dates / Nanny Share

Menu / Bottles

Meal	Description / Time

Sleeps

Name: From: To:

☐ Check every 10 min

Expenses

Price	Description

Toileting / Nappies

Activities / Outings

SUNSCREEN ☐

Observations / Reflections

INITIAL

| MONDAY ☑ | TUESDAY ☐ | WEDNESDAY ☐ | THURSDAY ☐ | FRIDAY ☐ | SATURDAY ☐ | SUNDAY ☐ |

Our Day

DATE: START TIME: FINISH:

Family Communication to Nanny / Educator

Notes to Family / Supplies Needed

Play Dates / Nanny Share

Menu / Bottles

Meal	Description / Time

Sleeps

Name:	From:	To:

☐ Check every 10 min

Expenses

Price	Description

Toileting / Nappies

Activities / Outings

SUNSCREEN ☐

Observations / Reflections

INITIAL

© Butter Diaries

| MONDAY ☑ | TUESDAY ☐ | WEDNESDAY ☐ | THURSDAY ☐ | FRIDAY ☐ | SATURDAY ☐ | SUNDAY ☐ |

Our Day

DATE: START TIME: FINISH:

Family Communication to Nanny / Educator

Notes to Family / Supplies Needed

Play Dates / Nanny Share

Menu / Bottles

Meal	Description / Time

Sleeps

Name: From: To:

☐ Check every 10 min

Expenses

Price	Description

Toileting / Nappies

Activities / Outings

SUNSCREEN ☐

Observations / Reflections

INITIAL

© Butler Diaries

| MONDAY ☑ | TUESDAY ☐ | WEDNESDAY ☐ | THURSDAY ☐ | FRIDAY ☐ | SATURDAY ☐ | SUNDAY ☐ |

Our Day

DATE:　　　　　　　START TIME:　　　　　　　FINISH:

Family Communication to Nanny / Educator

Notes to Family / Supplies Needed

Play Dates / Nanny Share

Menu / Bottles
Meal	Description / Time

Sleeps
Name:　　From:　　To:

☐ Check every 10 min

Expenses
Price	Description

Toileting / Nappies

Activities / Outings

SUNSCREEN ☐

Observations / Reflections

INITIAL

| MONDAY ☑ | TUESDAY ☐ | WEDNESDAY ☐ | THURSDAY ☐ | FRIDAY ☐ | SATURDAY ☐ | SUNDAY ☐ |

Our Day

DATE: START TIME: FINISH:

Family Communication to Nanny / Educator

Notes to Family / Supplies Needed

Play Dates / Nanny Share

Menu / Bottles

Meal	Description / Time

Sleeps

Name: From: To:

☐ Check every 10 min

Expenses

Price	Description

Toileting / Nappies

Activities / Outings

SUNSCREEN ☐

Observations / Reflections

INITIAL

| MONDAY ☑ | TUESDAY ☐ | WEDNESDAY ☐ | THURSDAY ☐ | FRIDAY ☐ | SATURDAY ☐ | SUNDAY ☐ |

Our Day

DATE: START TIME: FINISH:

Family Communication to Nanny / Educator

Notes to Family / Supplies Needed

Play Dates / Nanny Share

Menu / Bottles
Meal | Description / Time

Sleeps
Name: From: To:

☐ Check every 10 min

Expenses
Price | Description

Toileting / Nappies

Activities / Outings
SUNSCREEN ☐

Observations / Reflections

INITIAL

© Butler Diaries

| MONDAY ☑ | TUESDAY ☐ | WEDNESDAY ☐ | THURSDAY ☐ | FRIDAY ☐ | SATURDAY ☐ | SUNDAY ☐ |

Our Day

DATE: START TIME: FINISH:

Family Communication to Nanny / Educator

Notes to Family / Supplies Needed

Play Dates / Nanny Share

Menu / Bottles

Meal	Description / Time

Sleeps

Name: From: To:

☐ Check every 10 min

Expenses

Price	Description

Toileting / Nappies

Activities / Outings

SUNSCREEN ☐

Observations / Reflections

INITIAL

| MONDAY ☑ | TUESDAY ☐ | WEDNESDAY ☐ | THURSDAY ☐ | FRIDAY ☐ | SATURDAY ☐ | SUNDAY ☐ |

Our Day

DATE: START TIME: FINISH:

Family Communication to Nanny / Educator

Notes to Family / Supplies Needed

Play Dates / Nanny Share

Menu / Bottles

Meal	Description / Time

Sleeps

Name:	From:	To:

☐ Check every 10 min

Expenses

Price	Description

Toileting / Nappies

Activities / Outings

SUNSCREEN ☐

Observations / Reflections

INITIAL

© Butler Diaries

Our Day

☑ MONDAY ☐ TUESDAY ☐ WEDNESDAY ☐ THURSDAY ☐ FRIDAY ☐ SATURDAY ☐ SUNDAY

DATE: START TIME: FINISH:

Family Communication to Nanny / Educator

Notes to Family / Supplies Needed

Play Dates / Nanny Share

Menu / Bottles

Meal	Description / Time

Sleeps

Name: From: To:

☐ Check every 10 min

Expenses

Price	Description

Toileting / Nappies

Activities / Outings

☐ SUNSCREEN

Observations / Reflections

INITIAL

© Butler Diaries

| MONDAY ☑ | TUESDAY ☐ | WEDNESDAY ☐ | THURSDAY ☐ | FRIDAY ☐ | SATURDAY ☐ | SUNDAY ☐ |

Our Day

DATE: START TIME: FINISH:

Family Communication to Nanny / Educator

Notes to Family / Supplies Needed

Play Dates / Nanny Share

Menu / Bottles
Meal | Description / Time

Sleeps
Name: From: To:

☐ Check every 10 min

Expenses
Price | Description

Toileting / Nappies

Activities / Outings
SUNSCREEN ☐

Observations / Reflections

INITIAL

© Butler Diaries

| MONDAY ☑ | TUESDAY ☐ | WEDNESDAY ☐ | THURSDAY ☐ | FRIDAY ☐ | SATURDAY ☐ | SUNDAY ☐ |

Our Day

DATE: START TIME: FINISH:

Family Communication to Nanny / Educator

Notes to Family / Supplies Needed

Play Dates / Nanny Share

Menu / Bottles

Meal	Description / Time

Sleeps

Name: From: To:

☐ Check every 10 min

Expenses

Price	Description

Toileting / Nappies

Activities / Outings

SUNSCREEN ☐

Observations / Reflections

INITIAL

© Butler Diaries

| MONDAY ☑ | TUESDAY ☐ | WEDNESDAY ☐ | THURSDAY ☐ | FRIDAY ☐ | SATURDAY ☐ | SUNDAY ☐ |

Our Day

DATE: START TIME: FINISH:

Family Communication to Nanny / Educator

Notes to Family / Supplies Needed

Play Dates / Nanny Share

Menu / Bottles

Meal	Description / Time

Sleeps

Name:	From:	To:

☐ Check every 10 min

Expenses

Price	Description

Toileting / Nappies

Activities / Outings

SUNSCREEN ☐

Observations / Reflections

INITIAL

Our Day

MONDAY	TUESDAY	WEDNESDAY	THURSDAY	FRIDAY	SATURDAY	SUNDAY
☑	☐	☐	☐	☐	☐	☐

DATE: START TIME: FINISH:

Family Communication to Nanny / Educator

Notes to Family / Supplies Needed

Play Dates / Nanny Share

Menu / Bottles
Meal	Description / Time

Sleeps
Name: From: To:

☐ Check every 10 min

Expenses
Price	Description

Toileting / Nappies

Activities / Outings

SUNSCREEN ☐

Observations / Reflections

INITIAL

© Butler Diaries

| MONDAY ☑ | TUESDAY ☐ | WEDNESDAY ☐ | THURSDAY ☐ | FRIDAY ☐ | SATURDAY ☐ | SUNDAY ☐ |

Our Day

DATE: START TIME: FINISH:

Family Communication to Nanny / Educator

Notes to Family / Supplies Needed

Play Dates / Nanny Share

Menu / Bottles
Meal	Description / Time

Sleeps
Name: From: To:

☐ Check every 10 min

Expenses
Price	Description

Toileting / Nappies

Activities / Outings

SUNSCREEN ☐

Observations / Reflections

INITIAL

© Butler Diaries

Our Day

| MONDAY ☑ | TUESDAY ☐ | WEDNESDAY ☐ | THURSDAY ☐ | FRIDAY ☐ | SATURDAY ☐ | SUNDAY ☐ |

DATE: START TIME: FINISH:

Family Communication to Nanny / Educator

Notes to Family / Supplies Needed

Play Dates / Nanny Share

Menu / Bottles

Meal	Description / Time

Sleeps

Name: From: To:

☐ Check every 10 min

Expenses

Price	Description

Toileting / Nappies

Activities / Outings

SUNSCREEN ☐

Observations / Reflections

INITIAL

| MONDAY ☑ | TUESDAY ☐ | WEDNESDAY ☐ | THURSDAY ☐ | FRIDAY ☐ | SATURDAY ☐ | SUNDAY ☐ |

Our Day

DATE:	START TIME:	FINISH:

Family Communication to Nanny / Educator

Notes to Family / Supplies Needed

Play Dates / Nanny Share

Menu / Bottles
Meal	Description / Time

Sleeps
Name:	From:	To:

☐ Check every 10 min

Expenses
Price	Description

Toileting / Nappies

Activities / Outings

☐ SUNSCREEN

Observations / Reflections

INITIAL

© Butler Diaries

MONDAY ☑ TUESDAY ☐ WEDNESDAY ☐ THURSDAY ☐ FRIDAY ☐ SATURDAY ☐ SUNDAY ☐

Our Day

DATE: START TIME: FINISH:

Family Communication to Nanny / Educator

Notes to Family / Supplies Needed

Play Dates / Nanny Share

Menu / Bottles
Meal	Description / Time

Sleeps
Name: From: To:

☐ Check every 10 min

Expenses
Price	Description

Toileting / Nappies

Activities / Outings

SUNSCREEN ☐

Observations / Reflections

INITIAL

© Butter Diaries

MONDAY ☑ TUESDAY ☐ WEDNESDAY ☐ THURSDAY ☐ FRIDAY ☐ SATURDAY ☐ SUNDAY ☐

Our Day

DATE: START TIME: FINISH:

Family Communication to Nanny / Educator

Notes to Family / Supplies Needed

Play Dates / Nanny Share

Menu / Bottles
Meal | Description / Time

Sleeps
Name: From: To:

☐ Check every 10 min

Expenses
Price | Description

Toileting / Nappies

Activities / Outings

SUNSCREEN ☐

Observations / Reflections

INITIAL

© Butler Diaries

Our Day

| MONDAY ☑ | TUESDAY ☐ | WEDNESDAY ☐ | THURSDAY ☐ | FRIDAY ☐ | SATURDAY ☐ | SUNDAY ☐ |

DATE: START TIME: FINISH:

Family Communication to Nanny / Educator

Notes to Family / Supplies Needed

Play Dates / Nanny Share

Menu / Bottles

Meal	Description / Time

Sleeps

Name: From: To:

☐ Check every 10 min

Expenses

Price	Description

Toileting / Nappies

Activities / Outings

SUNSCREEN ☐

Observations / Reflections

INITIAL

| MONDAY ☑ | TUESDAY ☐ | WEDNESDAY ☐ | THURSDAY ☐ | FRIDAY ☐ | SATURDAY ☐ | SUNDAY ☐ |

Our Day

DATE: START TIME: FINISH:

Family Communication to Nanny / Educator

Notes to Family / Supplies Needed

Play Dates / Nanny Share

Menu / Bottles
Meal	Description / Time

Sleeps
Name: From: To:

☐ Check every 10 min

Expenses
Price	Description

Toileting / Nappies

Activities / Outings

SUNSCREEN ☐

Observations / Reflections

INITIAL

© Butler Diaries

Our Day

| MONDAY ☑ | TUESDAY ☐ | WEDNESDAY ☐ | THURSDAY ☐ | FRIDAY ☐ | SATURDAY ☐ | SUNDAY ☐ |

DATE: START TIME: FINISH:

Family Communication to Nanny / Educator

Notes to Family / Supplies Needed

Play Dates / Nanny Share

Menu / Bottles

Meal	Description / Time

Sleeps

Name: From: To:

☐ Check every 10 min

Expenses

Price	Description

Toileting / Nappies

Activities / Outings

SUNSCREEN ☐

Observations / Reflections

INITIAL

© Butler Diaries

| MONDAY ☑ | TUESDAY ☐ | WEDNESDAY ☐ | THURSDAY ☐ | FRIDAY ☐ | SATURDAY ☐ | SUNDAY ☐ |

Our Day

DATE: START TIME: FINISH:

Family Communication to Nanny / Educator

Notes to Family / Supplies Needed

Play Dates / Nanny Share

Menu / Bottles

Meal	Description / Time

Sleeps

Name: From: To:

☐ Check every 10 min

Expenses

Price	Description

Toileting / Nappies

Activities / Outings

SUNSCREEN ☐

Observations / Reflections

INITIAL

© Butler Diaries

Our Day

| MONDAY ☑ | TUESDAY ☐ | WEDNESDAY ☐ | THURSDAY ☐ | FRIDAY ☐ | SATURDAY ☐ | SUNDAY ☐ |

DATE: START TIME: FINISH:

Family Communication to Nanny / Educator

Notes to Family / Supplies Needed

Play Dates / Nanny Share

Menu / Bottles
Meal	Description / Time

Sleeps
Name: From: To:

☐ Check every 10 min

Expenses
Price	Description

Toileting / Nappies

Activities / Outings

SUNSCREEN ☐

Observations / Reflections

INITIAL

© Butter Diaries

| MONDAY ☑ | TUESDAY ☐ | WEDNESDAY ☐ | THURSDAY ☐ | FRIDAY ☐ | SATURDAY ☐ | SUNDAY ☐ |

Our Day

DATE: START TIME: FINISH:

Family Communication to Nanny / Educator

Notes to Family / Supplies Needed

Play Dates / Nanny Share

Menu / Bottles

Meal	Description / Time

Sleeps

Name: From: To:

☐ Check every 10 min

Expenses

Price	Description

Toileting / Nappies

Activities / Outings

☐ SUNSCREEN

Observations / Reflections

INITIAL

© Butler Diaries

| MONDAY ☑ | TUESDAY ☐ | WEDNESDAY ☐ | THURSDAY ☐ | FRIDAY ☐ | SATURDAY ☐ | SUNDAY ☐ |

Our Day

DATE: START TIME: FINISH:

Family Communication to Nanny / Educator

Notes to Family / Supplies Needed

Play Dates / Nanny Share

Menu / Bottles
Meal	Description / Time

Sleeps
Name: From: To:

☐ Check every 10 min

Expenses
Price	Description

Toileting / Nappies

Activities / Outings

SUNSCREEN ☐

Observations / Reflections

INITIAL

Our Day

MONDAY	TUESDAY	WEDNESDAY	THURSDAY	FRIDAY	SATURDAY	SUNDAY
☑	☐	☐	☐	☐	☐	☐

DATE: START TIME: FINISH:

Family Communication to Nanny / Educator

Notes to Family / Supplies Needed

Play Dates / Nanny Share

Menu / Bottles

Meal	Description / Time

Sleeps

Name: From: To:

☐ Check every 10 min

Expenses

Price	Description

Toileting / Nappies

Activities / Outings

SUNSCREEN ☐

Observations / Reflections

INITIAL

© Butter Diaries

| MONDAY ☑ | TUESDAY ☐ | WEDNESDAY ☐ | THURSDAY ☐ | FRIDAY ☐ | SATURDAY ☐ | SUNDAY ☐ |

Our Day

DATE: START TIME: FINISH:

Family Communication to Nanny / Educator

Notes to Family / Supplies Needed

Play Dates / Nanny Share

Menu / Bottles

Meal	Description / Time

Sleeps

Name: From: To:

☐ Check every 10 min

Expenses

Price	Description

Toileting / Nappies

Activities / Outings

SUNSCREEN ☐

Observations / Reflections

INITIAL

© Butter Diaries

| MONDAY ☑ | TUESDAY ☐ | WEDNESDAY ☐ | THURSDAY ☐ | FRIDAY ☐ | SATURDAY ☐ | SUNDAY ☐ |

Our Day

DATE: START TIME: FINISH:

Family Communication to Nanny / Educator

Notes to Family / Supplies Needed

Play Dates / Nanny Share

Menu / Bottles
Meal	Description / Time

Sleeps
Name: From: To:

☐ Check every 10 min

Expenses
Price	Description

Toileting / Nappies

Activities / Outings
☐ SUNSCREEN

Observations / Reflections

INITIAL

| MONDAY ☑ | TUESDAY ☐ | WEDNESDAY ☐ | THURSDAY ☐ | FRIDAY ☐ | SATURDAY ☐ | SUNDAY ☐ |

Our Day

DATE: START TIME: FINISH:

Family Communication to Nanny / Educator

Notes to Family / Supplies Needed

Play Dates / Nanny Share

Menu / Bottles

Meal	Description / Time

Sleeps

Name: From: To:

☐ Check every 10 min

Expenses

Price	Description

Toileting / Nappies

Activities / Outings

SUNSCREEN ☐

Observations / Reflections

INITIAL

Our Day

MONDAY	TUESDAY	WEDNESDAY	THURSDAY	FRIDAY	SATURDAY	SUNDAY
☑	☐	☐	☐	☐	☐	☐

DATE: START TIME: FINISH:

Family Communication to Nanny / Educator

Notes to Family / Supplies Needed

Play Dates / Nanny Share

Menu / Bottles

Meal	Description / Time

Sleeps

Name: From: To:

☐ Check every 10 min

Expenses

Price	Description

Toileting / Nappies

Activities / Outings

SUNSCREEN ☐

Observations / Reflections

INITIAL

Our Day

☑ MONDAY ☐ TUESDAY ☐ WEDNESDAY ☐ THURSDAY ☐ FRIDAY ☐ SATURDAY ☐ SUNDAY

DATE: START TIME: FINISH:

Family Communication to Nanny / Educator

Notes to Family / Supplies Needed

Play Dates / Nanny Share

Menu / Bottles

Meal	Description / Time

Sleeps

Name: From: To:

☐ Check every 10 min

Expenses

Price	Description

Toileting / Nappies

Activities / Outings

☐ SUNSCREEN

Observations / Reflections

INITIAL

© Butler Diaries

MONDAY	TUESDAY	WEDNESDAY	THURSDAY	FRIDAY	SATURDAY	SUNDAY
☑	☐	☐	☐	☐	☐	☐

Our Day

DATE: START TIME: FINISH:

Family Communication to Nanny / Educator

Notes to Family / Supplies Needed

Play Dates / Nanny Share

Menu / Bottles
Meal   Description / Time

Sleeps
Name: From: To:

☐ Check every 10 min

Expenses
Price   Description

Toileting / Nappies

Activities / Outings
SUNSCREEN ☐

Observations / Reflections

INITIAL

© Butler Diaries

Our Day

MONDAY ☑ TUESDAY ☐ WEDNESDAY ☐ THURSDAY ☐ FRIDAY ☐ SATURDAY ☐ SUNDAY ☐

DATE: START TIME: FINISH:

Family Communication to Nanny / Educator

Notes to Family / Supplies Needed

Play Dates / Nanny Share

Menu / Bottles

Meal	Description / Time

Sleeps

Name: From: To:

☐ Check every 10 min

Expenses

Price	Description

Toileting / Nappies

Activities / Outings

SUNSCREEN ☐

Observations / Reflections

INITIAL

| MONDAY ☑ | TUESDAY ☐ | WEDNESDAY ☐ | THURSDAY ☐ | FRIDAY ☐ | SATURDAY ☐ | SUNDAY ☐ |

Our Day

DATE: START TIME: FINISH:

Family Communication to Nanny / Educator

Notes to Family / Supplies Needed

Play Dates / Nanny Share

Menu / Bottles

Meal	Description / Time

Sleeps

Name: From: To:

☐ Check every 10 min

Expenses

Price	Description

Toileting / Nappies

Activities / Outings

SUNSCREEN ☐

Observations / Reflections

INITIAL

© Butler Diaries

| MONDAY ☑ | TUESDAY ☐ | WEDNESDAY ☐ | THURSDAY ☐ | FRIDAY ☐ | SATURDAY ☐ | SUNDAY ☐ |

Our Day

DATE: START TIME: FINISH:

Family Communication to Nanny / Educator

Notes to Family / Supplies Needed

Play Dates / Nanny Share

Menu / Bottles
Meal	Description / Time

Sleeps
Name: From: To:

☐ Check every 10 min

Expenses
Price	Description

Toileting / Nappies

Activities / Outings

SUNSCREEN ☐

Observations / Reflections

INITIAL

© Butter Diaries

MONDAY	TUESDAY	WEDNESDAY	THURSDAY	FRIDAY	SATURDAY	SUNDAY
☑	☐	☐	☐	☐	☐	☐

Our Day

DATE: START TIME: FINISH:

Family Communication to Nanny / Educator

Notes to Family / Supplies Needed

Play Dates / Nanny Share

Menu / Bottles
Meal	Description / Time

Sleeps
Name: From: To:

☐ Check every 10 min

Expenses
Price	Description

Toileting / Nappies

Activities / Outings

SUNSCREEN ☐

Observations / Reflections

INITIAL

© Butler Diaries

| MONDAY ☑ | TUESDAY ☐ | WEDNESDAY ☐ | THURSDAY ☐ | FRIDAY ☐ | SATURDAY ☐ | SUNDAY ☐ |

Our Day

DATE: START TIME: FINISH:

Family Communication to Nanny / Educator

Notes to Family / Supplies Needed

Play Dates / Nanny Share

Menu / Bottles

Meal	Description / Time

Sleeps

Name: From: To:

☐ Check every 10 min

Expenses

Price	Description

Toileting / Nappies

Activities / Outings

SUNSCREEN ☐

Observations / Reflections

INITIAL

© Butter Diaries

| MONDAY ☑ | TUESDAY ☐ | WEDNESDAY ☐ | THURSDAY ☐ | FRIDAY ☐ | SATURDAY ☐ | SUNDAY ☐ |

Our Day

DATE: START TIME: FINISH:

Family Communication to Nanny / Educator

Notes to Family / Supplies Needed

Play Dates / Nanny Share

Menu / Bottles

Meal	Description / Time

Sleeps

Name: From: To:

☐ Check every 10 min

Expenses

Price	Description

Toileting / Nappies

Activities / Outings

SUNSCREEN ☐

Observations / Reflections

INITIAL

Our Day

| MONDAY ☑ | TUESDAY ☐ | WEDNESDAY ☐ | THURSDAY ☐ | FRIDAY ☐ | SATURDAY ☐ | SUNDAY ☐ |

DATE: START TIME: FINISH:

Family Communication to Nanny / Educator

Notes to Family / Supplies Needed

Play Dates / Nanny Share

Menu / Bottles

Meal	Description / Time

Sleeps

Name: From: To:

☐ Check every 10 min

Expenses

Price	Description

Toileting / Nappies

Activities / Outings

SUNSCREEN ☐

Observations / Reflections

INITIAL

| MONDAY ☑ | TUESDAY ☐ | WEDNESDAY ☐ | THURSDAY ☐ | FRIDAY ☐ | SATURDAY ☐ | SUNDAY ☐ |

Our Day

DATE: START TIME: FINISH:

Family Communication to Nanny / Educator

Notes to Family / Supplies Needed

Play Dates / Nanny Share

Menu / Bottles
Meal | Description / Time

Sleeps
Name: From: To:

☐ Check every 10 min

Expenses
Price | Description

Toileting / Nappies

Activities / Outings

SUNSCREEN ☐

Observations / Reflections

INITIAL

© Butler Diaries

Our Day

| MONDAY ☑ | TUESDAY ☐ | WEDNESDAY ☐ | THURSDAY ☐ | FRIDAY ☐ | SATURDAY ☐ | SUNDAY ☐ |

DATE: START TIME: FINISH:

Family Communication to Nanny / Educator

Notes to Family / Supplies Needed

Play Dates / Nanny Share

Menu / Bottles

Meal	Description / Time

Sleeps

Name: From: To:

☐ Check every 10 min

Expenses

Price	Description

Toileting / Nappies

Activities / Outings

SUNSCREEN ☐

Observations / Reflections

INITIAL

© Butler Diaries

| MONDAY ☑ | TUESDAY ☐ | WEDNESDAY ☐ | THURSDAY ☐ | FRIDAY ☐ | SATURDAY ☐ | SUNDAY ☐ |

Our Day

DATE: START TIME: FINISH:

Family Communication to Nanny / Educator

Notes to Family / Supplies Needed

Play Dates / Nanny Share

Menu / Bottles
Meal	Description / Time

Sleeps
Name: From: To:

☐ Check every 10 min

Expenses
Price	Description

Toileting / Nappies

Activities / Outings

SUNSCREEN ☐

Observations / Reflections

INITIAL

© Butler Diaries

Our Day

| ☑ MONDAY | ☐ TUESDAY | ☐ WEDNESDAY | ☐ THURSDAY | ☐ FRIDAY | ☐ SATURDAY | ☐ SUNDAY |

DATE: START TIME: FINISH:

Family Communication to Nanny / Educator

Notes to Family / Supplies Needed

Play Dates / Nanny Share

Menu / Bottles

Meal	Description / Time

Sleeps

Name:	From:	To:

☐ Check every 10 min

Expenses

Price	Description

Toileting / Nappies

Activities / Outings

☐ SUNSCREEN

Observations / Reflections

INITIAL

MONDAY	TUESDAY	WEDNESDAY	THURSDAY	FRIDAY	SATURDAY	SUNDAY
☑	☐	☐	☐	☐	☐	☐

Our Day

DATE: START TIME: FINISH:

Family Communication to Nanny / Educator

Notes to Family / Supplies Needed

Play Dates / Nanny Share

Menu / Bottles

Meal	Description / Time

Sleeps

Name: From: To:

☐ Check every 10 min

Expenses

Price	Description

Toileting / Nappies

Activities / Outings

SUNSCREEN ☐

Observations / Reflections

INITIAL

Our Day

MONDAY	TUESDAY	WEDNESDAY	THURSDAY	FRIDAY	SATURDAY	SUNDAY
☑	☐	☐	☐	☐	☐	☐

DATE: START TIME: FINISH:

Family Communication to Nanny / Educator

Notes to Family / Supplies Needed

Play Dates / Nanny Share

Menu / Bottles

Meal	Description / Time

Sleeps

Name: From: To:

☐ Check every 10 min

Expenses

Price	Description

Toileting / Nappies

Activities / Outings   SUNSCREEN ☐

Observations / Reflections

INITIAL

MONDAY ☑ TUESDAY ☐ WEDNESDAY ☐ THURSDAY ☐ FRIDAY ☐ SATURDAY ☐ SUNDAY ☐

Our Day

DATE: START TIME: FINISH:

Family Communication to Nanny / Educator

Notes to Family / Supplies Needed

Play Dates / Nanny Share

Menu / Bottles

Meal	Description / Time

Sleeps

Name: From: To:

☐ Check every 10 min

Expenses

Price	Description

Toileting / Nappies

Activities / Outings

SUNSCREEN ☐

Observations / Reflections

INITIAL

© Butler Diaries

| MONDAY ☑ | TUESDAY ☐ | WEDNESDAY ☐ | THURSDAY ☐ | FRIDAY ☐ | SATURDAY ☐ | SUNDAY ☐ |

Our Day

DATE:　　　　　　　START TIME:　　　　　　　FINISH:

Family Communication to Nanny / Educator

Notes to Family / Supplies Needed

Play Dates / Nanny Share

Menu / Bottles

Meal	Description / Time

Sleeps

Name:　　From:　　To:

☐ Check every 10 min

Expenses

Price	Description

Toileting / Nappies

Activities / Outings

SUNSCREEN ☐

Observations / Reflections

INITIAL

Our Day

| MONDAY ☑ | TUESDAY ☐ | WEDNESDAY ☐ | THURSDAY ☐ | FRIDAY ☐ | SATURDAY ☐ | SUNDAY ☐ |

DATE: START TIME: FINISH:

Family Communication to Nanny / Educator

Notes to Family / Supplies Needed

Play Dates / Nanny Share

Menu / Bottles
Meal	Description / Time

Sleeps
Name: From: To:

☐ Check every 10 min

Expenses
Price	Description

Toileting / Nappies

Activities / Outings

SUNSCREEN ☐

Observations / Reflections

INITIAL

© Butler Diaries

| MONDAY ☑ | TUESDAY ☐ | WEDNESDAY ☐ | THURSDAY ☐ | FRIDAY ☐ | SATURDAY ☐ | SUNDAY ☐ |

Our Day

DATE: START TIME: FINISH:

Family Communication to Nanny / Educator

Notes to Family / Supplies Needed

Play Dates / Nanny Share

Menu / Bottles
Meal	Description / Time

Sleeps
Name: From: To:

☐ Check every 10 min

Expenses
Price	Description

Toileting / Nappies

Activities / Outings

SUNSCREEN ☐

Observations / Reflections

INITIAL

© Butter Diaries

| MONDAY ☑ | TUESDAY ☐ | WEDNESDAY ☐ | THURSDAY ☐ | FRIDAY ☐ | SATURDAY ☐ | SUNDAY ☐ |

Our Day

DATE: START TIME: FINISH:

Family Communication to Nanny / Educator

Notes to Family / Supplies Needed

Play Dates / Nanny Share

Menu / Bottles
Meal	Description / Time

Sleeps
Name: From: To:

☐ Check every 10 min

Expenses
Price	Description

Toileting / Nappies

Activities / Outings

SUNSCREEN ☐

Observations / Reflections

INITIAL

© Butler Diaries

Our Day

MONDAY	TUESDAY	WEDNESDAY	THURSDAY	FRIDAY	SATURDAY	SUNDAY
☑	☐	☐	☐	☐	☐	☐

DATE: START TIME: FINISH:

Family Communication to Nanny / Educator

Notes to Family / Supplies Needed

Play Dates / Nanny Share

Menu / Bottles

Meal	Description / Time

Sleeps

Name: From: To:

☐ Check every 10 min

Expenses

Price	Description

Toileting / Nappies

Activities / Outings

SUNSCREEN ☐

Observations / Reflections

INITIAL

Our Day

MONDAY	TUESDAY	WEDNESDAY	THURSDAY	FRIDAY	SATURDAY	SUNDAY
☑	☐	☐	☐	☐	☐	☐

DATE: START TIME: FINISH:

Family Communication to Nanny / Educator

Notes to Family / Supplies Needed

Play Dates / Nanny Share

Menu / Bottles

Meal	Description / Time

Sleeps

Name: From: To:

☐ Check every 10 min

Expenses

Price	Description

Toileting / Nappies

Activities / Outings

SUNSCREEN ☐

Observations / Reflections

INITIAL

| MONDAY ☑ | TUESDAY ☐ | WEDNESDAY ☐ | THURSDAY ☐ | FRIDAY ☐ | SATURDAY ☐ | SUNDAY ☐ |

Our Day

DATE: START TIME: FINISH:

Family Communication to Nanny / Educator

Notes to Family / Supplies Needed

Play Dates / Nanny Share

Menu / Bottles
Meal	Description / Time

Sleeps
Name: From: To:

☐ Check every 10 min

Expenses
Price	Description

Toileting / Nappies

Activities / Outings

SUNSCREEN ☐

Observations / Reflections

INITIAL

| MONDAY ☑ | TUESDAY ☐ | WEDNESDAY ☐ | THURSDAY ☐ | FRIDAY ☐ | SATURDAY ☐ | SUNDAY ☐ |

Our Day

DATE: START TIME: FINISH:

Family Communication to Nanny / Educator

Notes to Family / Supplies Needed

Play Dates / Nanny Share

Menu / Bottles
Meal	Description / Time

Sleeps
Name: From: To:

☐ Check every 10 min

Expenses
Price	Description

Toileting / Nappies

Activities / Outings

SUNSCREEN ☐

Observations / Reflections

INITIAL

| MONDAY ☑ | TUESDAY ☐ | WEDNESDAY ☐ | THURSDAY ☐ | FRIDAY ☐ | SATURDAY ☐ | SUNDAY ☐ |

Our Day

DATE: START TIME: FINISH:

Family Communication to Nanny / Educator

Notes to Family / Supplies Needed

Play Dates / Nanny Share

Menu / Bottles
Meal	Description / Time

Sleeps
Name: From: To:

☐ Check every 10 min

Expenses
Price	Description

Toileting / Nappies

Activities / Outings   SUNSCREEN ☐

Observations / Reflections

INITIAL

© Butter Diaries

Our Day

| MONDAY ☑ | TUESDAY ☐ | WEDNESDAY ☐ | THURSDAY ☐ | FRIDAY ☐ | SATURDAY ☐ | SUNDAY ☐ |

DATE: START TIME: FINISH:

Family Communication to Nanny / Educator

Notes to Family / Supplies Needed

Play Dates / Nanny Share

Menu / Bottles
Meal	Description / Time

Sleeps
Name:	From:	To:

☐ Check every 10 min

Expenses
Price	Description

Toileting / Nappies

Activities / Outings

SUNSCREEN ☐

Observations / Reflections

INITIAL

© Butler Diaries

| MONDAY ☑ | TUESDAY ☐ | WEDNESDAY ☐ | THURSDAY ☐ | FRIDAY ☐ | SATURDAY ☐ | SUNDAY ☐ |

Our Day

DATE: START TIME: FINISH:

Family Communication to Nanny / Educator

Notes to Family / Supplies Needed

Play Dates / Nanny Share

Menu / Bottles

Meal	Description / Time

Sleeps

Name: From: To:

☐ Check every 10 min

Expenses

Price	Description

Toileting / Nappies

Activities / Outings

SUNSCREEN ☐

Observations / Reflections

INITIAL

MONDAY	TUESDAY	WEDNESDAY	THURSDAY	FRIDAY	SATURDAY	SUNDAY
☑	☐	☐	☐	☐	☐	☐

Our Day

DATE: START TIME: FINISH:

Family Communication to Nanny / Educator

Notes to Family / Supplies Needed

Play Dates / Nanny Share

Menu / Bottles
Meal	Description / Time

Sleeps
Name: From: To:

☐ Check every 10 min

Expenses
Price	Description

Toileting / Nappies

Activities / Outings

SUNSCREEN ☐

Observations / Reflections

INITIAL

Our Day

MONDAY	TUESDAY	WEDNESDAY	THURSDAY	FRIDAY	SATURDAY	SUNDAY
☑	☐	☐	☐	☐	☐	☐

DATE: START TIME: FINISH:

Family Communication to Nanny / Educator

Notes to Family / Supplies Needed

Play Dates / Nanny Share

Menu / Bottles

Meal	Description / Time

Sleeps

Name: From: To:

☐ Check every 10 min

Expenses

Price	Description

Toileting / Nappies

Activities / Outings

SUNSCREEN ☐

Observations / Reflections

INITIAL

| MONDAY ☑ | TUESDAY ☐ | WEDNESDAY ☐ | THURSDAY ☐ | FRIDAY ☐ | SATURDAY ☐ | SUNDAY ☐ |

Our Day

DATE: START TIME: FINISH:

Family Communication to Nanny / Educator

Notes to Family / Supplies Needed

Play Dates / Nanny Share

Menu / Bottles
Meal	Description / Time

Sleeps
Name: From: To:

☐ Check every 10 min

Expenses
Price	Description

Toileting / Nappies

Activities / Outings

SUNSCREEN ☐

Observations / Reflections

INITIAL

| MONDAY ☑ | TUESDAY ☐ | WEDNESDAY ☐ | THURSDAY ☐ | FRIDAY ☐ | SATURDAY ☐ | SUNDAY ☐ |

Our Day

DATE: START TIME: FINISH:

Family Communication to Nanny / Educator

Notes to Family / Supplies Needed

Play Dates / Nanny Share

Menu / Bottles

Meal	Description / Time

Sleeps

Name: From: To:

☐ Check every 10 min

Expenses

Price	Description

Toileting / Nappies

Activities / Outings

SUNSCREEN ☐

Observations / Reflections

INITIAL

| MONDAY ☑ | TUESDAY ☐ | WEDNESDAY ☐ | THURSDAY ☐ | FRIDAY ☐ | SATURDAY ☐ | SUNDAY ☐ |

Our Day

DATE: START TIME: FINISH:

Family Communication to Nanny / Educator

Notes to Family / Supplies Needed

Play Dates / Nanny Share

Menu / Bottles

Meal	Description / Time

Sleeps

Name: From: To:

☐ Check every 10 min

Expenses

Price	Description

Toileting / Nappies

Activities / Outings

SUNSCREEN ☐

Observations / Reflections

INITIAL

| MONDAY ☑ | TUESDAY ☐ | WEDNESDAY ☐ | THURSDAY ☐ | FRIDAY ☐ | SATURDAY ☐ | SUNDAY ☐ |

Our Day

DATE: START TIME: FINISH:

Family Communication to Nanny / Educator

Notes to Family / Supplies Needed

Play Dates / Nanny Share

Menu / Bottles

Meal	Description / Time

Sleeps

Name: From: To:

☐ Check every 10 min

Expenses

Price	Description

Toileting / Nappies

Activities / Outings

SUNSCREEN ☐

Observations / Reflections

INITIAL

© Butter Diaries

Our Day

| MONDAY ☑ | TUESDAY ☐ | WEDNESDAY ☐ | THURSDAY ☐ | FRIDAY ☐ | SATURDAY ☐ | SUNDAY ☐ |

DATE: START TIME: FINISH:

Family Communication to Nanny / Educator

Notes to Family / Supplies Needed

Play Dates / Nanny Share

Menu / Bottles

Meal	Description / Time

Sleeps

Name: From: To:

☐ Check every 10 min

Expenses

Price	Description

Toileting / Nappies

Activities / Outings

SUNSCREEN ☐

Observations / Reflections

INITIAL

© Butler Diaries

Our Day

| MONDAY ☑ | TUESDAY ☐ | WEDNESDAY ☐ | THURSDAY ☐ | FRIDAY ☐ | SATURDAY ☐ | SUNDAY ☐ |

DATE: START TIME: FINISH:

Family Communication to Nanny / Educator

Notes to Family / Supplies Needed

Play Dates / Nanny Share

Menu / Bottles

Meal	Description / Time

Sleeps

Name: From: To:

☐ Check every 10 min

Expenses

Price	Description

Toileting / Nappies

Activities / Outings

SUNSCREEN ☐

Observations / Reflections

INITIAL

Our Day

- [x] MONDAY
- [ ] TUESDAY
- [ ] WEDNESDAY
- [ ] THURSDAY
- [ ] FRIDAY
- [ ] SATURDAY
- [ ] SUNDAY

DATE: START TIME: FINISH:

Family Communication to Nanny / Educator

Notes to Family / Supplies Needed

Play Dates / Nanny Share

Menu / Bottles

Meal	Description / Time

Sleeps

Name: From: To:

- [ ] Check every 10 min

Expenses

Price	Description

Toileting / Nappies

Activities / Outings

- [ ] SUNSCREEN

Observations / Reflections

INITIAL

Our Day

☑ MONDAY ☐ TUESDAY ☐ WEDNESDAY ☐ THURSDAY ☐ FRIDAY ☐ SATURDAY ☐ SUNDAY

DATE: START TIME: FINISH:

Family Communication to Nanny / Educator

Notes to Family / Supplies Needed

Play Dates / Nanny Share

Menu / Bottles
Meal	Description / Time

Sleeps
Name: From: To:

☐ Check every 10 min

Expenses
Price	Description

Toileting / Nappies

Activities / Outings

☐ SUNSCREEN

Observations / Reflections

INITIAL

© Butler Diaries

MONDAY ☑ TUESDAY ☐ WEDNESDAY ☐ THURSDAY ☐ FRIDAY ☐ SATURDAY ☐ SUNDAY ☐

Our Day

DATE: START TIME: FINISH:

Family Communication to Nanny / Educator

Notes to Family / Supplies Needed

Play Dates / Nanny Share

Menu / Bottles

Meal	Description / Time

Sleeps

Name: From: To:

☐ Check every 10 min

Expenses

Price	Description

Toileting / Nappies

Activities / Outings

SUNSCREEN ☐

Observations / Reflections

INITIAL

| MONDAY ☑ | TUESDAY ☐ | WEDNESDAY ☐ | THURSDAY ☐ | FRIDAY ☐ | SATURDAY ☐ | SUNDAY ☐ |

Our Day

DATE: START TIME: FINISH:

Family Communication to Nanny / Educator

Notes to Family / Supplies Needed

Play Dates / Nanny Share

Menu / Bottles

Meal	Description / Time

Sleeps

Name: From: To:

☐ Check every 10 min

Expenses

Price	Description

Toileting / Nappies

Activities / Outings

SUNSCREEN ☐

Observations / Reflections

INITIAL

| MONDAY ☑ | TUESDAY ☐ | WEDNESDAY ☐ | THURSDAY ☐ | FRIDAY ☐ | SATURDAY ☐ | SUNDAY ☐ |

Our Day

DATE: START TIME: FINISH:

Family Communication to Nanny / Educator

Notes to Family / Supplies Needed

Play Dates / Nanny Share

Menu / Bottles
Meal | Description / Time

Sleeps
Name: From: To:

☐ Check every 10 min

Expenses
Price | Description

Toileting / Nappies

Activities / Outings
SUNSCREEN ☐

Observations / Reflections

INITIAL

© Butler Diaries

| MONDAY ☑ | TUESDAY ☐ | WEDNESDAY ☐ | THURSDAY ☐ | FRIDAY ☐ | SATURDAY ☐ | SUNDAY ☐ |

Our Day

DATE: START TIME: FINISH:

Family Communication to Nanny / Educator

Notes to Family / Supplies Needed

Play Dates / Nanny Share

Menu / Bottles

Meal	Description / Time

Sleeps

Name: From: To:

☐ Check every 10 min

Expenses

Price	Description

Toileting / Nappies

Activities / Outings

SUNSCREEN ☐

Observations / Reflections

INITIAL

Our Day

| MONDAY ☑ | TUESDAY ☐ | WEDNESDAY ☐ | THURSDAY ☐ | FRIDAY ☐ | SATURDAY ☐ | SUNDAY ☐ |

DATE: START TIME: FINISH:

Family Communication to Nanny / Educator

Notes to Family / Supplies Needed

Play Dates / Nanny Share

Menu / Bottles

Meal	Description / Time

Sleeps

Name: From: To:

☐ Check every 10 min

Expenses

Price	Description

Toileting / Nappies

Activities / Outings

SUNSCREEN ☐

Observations / Reflections

INITIAL

Our Day

MONDAY	TUESDAY	WEDNESDAY	THURSDAY	FRIDAY	SATURDAY	SUNDAY
☑	☐	☐	☐	☐	☐	☐

DATE: START TIME: FINISH:

Family Communication to Nanny / Educator

Notes to Family / Supplies Needed

Play Dates / Nanny Share

Menu / Bottles

Meal	Description / Time

Sleeps

Name: From: To:

☐ Check every 10 min

Expenses

Price	Description

Toileting / Nappies

Activities / Outings

☐ SUNSCREEN

Observations / Reflections

INITIAL

© Butler Diaries

| MONDAY ☑ | TUESDAY ☐ | WEDNESDAY ☐ | THURSDAY ☐ | FRIDAY ☐ | SATURDAY ☐ | SUNDAY ☐ |

Our Day

DATE: START TIME: FINISH:

Family Communication to Nanny / Educator

Notes to Family / Supplies Needed

Play Dates / Nanny Share

Menu / Bottles
Meal	Description / Time

Sleeps
Name:	From:	To:

☐ Check every 10 min

Expenses
Price	Description

Toileting / Nappies

Activities / Outings

SUNSCREEN ☐

Observations / Reflections

INITIAL

© Butter Diaries

Our Day

| MONDAY ☑ | TUESDAY ☐ | WEDNESDAY ☐ | THURSDAY ☐ | FRIDAY ☐ | SATURDAY ☐ | SUNDAY ☐ |

DATE: START TIME: FINISH:

Family Communication to Nanny / Educator

Notes to Family / Supplies Needed

Play Dates / Nanny Share

Menu / Bottles

Meal	Description / Time

Sleeps

Name:	From:	To:

☐ Check every 10 min

Expenses

Price	Description

Toileting / Nappies

Activities / Outings

☐ SUNSCREEN

Observations / Reflections

INITIAL

MONDAY ☑ TUESDAY ☐ WEDNESDAY ☐ THURSDAY ☐ FRIDAY ☐ SATURDAY ☐ SUNDAY ☐

Our Day

DATE: START TIME: FINISH:

Family Communication to Nanny / Educator

Notes to Family / Supplies Needed

Play Dates / Nanny Share

Menu / Bottles
Meal	Description / Time

Sleeps
Name: From: To:

☐ Check every 10 min

Expenses
Price	Description

Toileting / Nappies

Activities / Outings

SUNSCREEN ☐

Observations / Reflections

INITIAL

© Butler Diaries

Our Day

☑ MONDAY ☐ TUESDAY ☐ WEDNESDAY ☐ THURSDAY ☐ FRIDAY ☐ SATURDAY ☐ SUNDAY

DATE: START TIME: FINISH:

Family Communication to Nanny / Educator

Notes to Family / Supplies Needed

Play Dates / Nanny Share

Menu / Bottles

Meal	Description / Time

Sleeps

Name: From: To:

☐ Check every 10 min

Expenses

Price	Description

Toileting / Nappies

Activities / Outings

SUNSCREEN ☐

Observations / Reflections

INITIAL

| MONDAY ☑ | TUESDAY ☐ | WEDNESDAY ☐ | THURSDAY ☐ | FRIDAY ☐ | SATURDAY ☐ | SUNDAY ☐ |

Our Day

DATE: START TIME: FINISH:

Family Communication to Nanny / Educator

Notes to Family / Supplies Needed

Play Dates / Nanny Share

Menu / Bottles
Meal	Description / Time

Sleeps
Name: From: To:

☐ Check every 10 min

Expenses
Price	Description

Toileting / Nappies

Activities / Outings

SUNSCREEN ☐

Observations / Reflections

INITIAL

Our Day

| MONDAY ☑ | TUESDAY ☐ | WEDNESDAY ☐ | THURSDAY ☐ | FRIDAY ☐ | SATURDAY ☐ | SUNDAY ☐ |

DATE: START TIME: FINISH:

Family Communication to Nanny / Educator

Notes to Family / Supplies Needed

Play Dates / Nanny Share

Menu / Bottles
Meal	Description / Time

Sleeps
Name: From: To:

☐ Check every 10 min

Expenses
Price	Description

Toileting / Nappies

Activities / Outings

SUNSCREEN ☐

Observations / Reflections

INITIAL

| MONDAY ☑ | TUESDAY ☐ | WEDNESDAY ☐ | THURSDAY ☐ | FRIDAY ☐ | SATURDAY ☐ | SUNDAY ☐ |

Our Day

DATE: START TIME: FINISH:

Family Communication to Nanny / Educator

Notes to Family / Supplies Needed

Play Dates / Nanny Share

Menu / Bottles

Meal	Description / Time

Sleeps

Name: From: To:

☐ Check every 10 min

Expenses

Price	Description

Toileting / Nappies

Activities / Outings

SUNSCREEN ☐

Observations / Reflections

INITIAL

| MONDAY ☑ | TUESDAY ☐ | WEDNESDAY ☐ | THURSDAY ☐ | FRIDAY ☐ | SATURDAY ☐ | SUNDAY ☐ |

Our Day

DATE: START TIME: FINISH:

Family Communication to Nanny / Educator

Notes to Family / Supplies Needed

Play Dates / Nanny Share

Menu / Bottles

Meal	Description / Time

Sleeps

Name: From: To:

☐ Check every 10 min

Expenses

Price	Description

Toileting / Nappies

Activities / Outings

SUNSCREEN ☐

Observations / Reflections

INITIAL

| MONDAY ☑ | TUESDAY ☐ | WEDNESDAY ☐ | THURSDAY ☐ | FRIDAY ☐ | SATURDAY ☐ | SUNDAY ☐ |

Our Day

DATE: START TIME: FINISH:

Family Communication to Nanny / Educator

Notes to Family / Supplies Needed

Play Dates / Nanny Share

Menu / Bottles
Meal	Description / Time

Sleeps
Name: From: To:

☐ Check every 10 min

Expenses
Price	Description

Toileting / Nappies

Activities / Outings

SUNSCREEN ☐

Observations / Reflections

INITIAL

| MONDAY ☑ | TUESDAY ☐ | WEDNESDAY ☐ | THURSDAY ☐ | FRIDAY ☐ | SATURDAY ☐ | SUNDAY ☐ |

Our Day

DATE: START TIME: FINISH:

Family Communication to Nanny / Educator

Notes to Family / Supplies Needed

Play Dates / Nanny Share

Menu / Bottles
Meal	Description / Time

Sleeps
Name: From: To:

☐ Check every 10 min

Expenses
Price	Description

Toileting / Nappies

Activities / Outings

SUNSCREEN ☐

Observations / Reflections

INITIAL

| MONDAY ☑ | TUESDAY ☐ | WEDNESDAY ☐ | THURSDAY ☐ | FRIDAY ☐ | SATURDAY ☐ | SUNDAY ☐ |

Our Day

DATE: START TIME: FINISH:

Family Communication to Nanny / Educator

Notes to Family / Supplies Needed

Play Dates / Nanny Share

Menu / Bottles
Meal   Description / Time

Sleeps
Name: From: To:

☐ Check every 10 min

Expenses
Price   Description

Toileting / Nappies

Activities / Outings
SUNSCREEN ☐

Observations / Reflections

INITIAL

© Butter Diaries

Our Day

MONDAY	TUESDAY	WEDNESDAY	THURSDAY	FRIDAY	SATURDAY	SUNDAY
☑	☐	☐	☐	☐	☐	☐

DATE: START TIME: FINISH:

Family Communication to Nanny / Educator

Notes to Family / Supplies Needed

Play Dates / Nanny Share

Menu / Bottles

Meal	Description / Time

Sleeps

Name: From: To:

☐ Check every 10 min

Expenses

Price	Description

Toileting / Nappies

Activities / Outings

SUNSCREEN ☐

Observations / Reflections

INITIAL

| MONDAY ☑ | TUESDAY ☐ | WEDNESDAY ☐ | THURSDAY ☐ | FRIDAY ☐ | SATURDAY ☐ | SUNDAY ☐ |

Our Day

DATE: START TIME: FINISH:

Family Communication to Nanny / Educator

Notes to Family / Supplies Needed

Play Dates / Nanny Share

Menu / Bottles
Meal | Description / Time

Sleeps
Name: From: To:

☐ Check every 10 min

Expenses
Price | Description

Toileting / Nappies

Activities / Outings
SUNSCREEN ☐

Observations / Reflections

INITIAL

© Butler Diaries

| MONDAY ☑ | TUESDAY ☐ | WEDNESDAY ☐ | THURSDAY ☐ | FRIDAY ☐ | SATURDAY ☐ | SUNDAY ☐ |

Our Day

DATE: START TIME: FINISH:

Family Communication to Nanny / Educator

Notes to Family / Supplies Needed

Play Dates / Nanny Share

Menu / Bottles

Meal	Description / Time

Sleeps

Name: From: To:

☐ Check every 10 min

Expenses

Price	Description

Toileting / Nappies

Activities / Outings

SUNSCREEN ☐

Observations / Reflections

INITIAL

Our Day

☑ MONDAY ☐ TUESDAY ☐ WEDNESDAY ☐ THURSDAY ☐ FRIDAY ☐ SATURDAY ☐ SUNDAY

DATE: START TIME: FINISH:

Family Communication to Nanny / Educator

Notes to Family / Supplies Needed

Play Dates / Nanny Share

Menu / Bottles

Meal	Description / Time

Sleeps

Name: From: To:

☐ Check every 10 min

Expenses

Price	Description

Toileting / Nappies

Activities / Outings

☐ SUNSCREEN

Observations / Reflections

INITIAL

© Butler Diaries

Our Day

| MONDAY ☑ | TUESDAY ☐ | WEDNESDAY ☐ | THURSDAY ☐ | FRIDAY ☐ | SATURDAY ☐ | SUNDAY ☐ |

DATE: START TIME: FINISH:

Family Communication to Nanny / Educator

Notes to Family / Supplies Needed

Play Dates / Nanny Share

Menu / Bottles

Meal	Description / Time

Sleeps

Name: From: To:

☐ Check every 10 min

Expenses

Price	Description

Toileting / Nappies

Activities / Outings

SUNSCREEN ☐

Observations / Reflections

INITIAL

© Butler Diaries

MONDAY	TUESDAY	WEDNESDAY	THURSDAY	FRIDAY	SATURDAY	SUNDAY
☑	☐	☐	☐	☐	☐	☐

Our Day

DATE: START TIME: FINISH:

Family Communication to Nanny / Educator

Notes to Family / Supplies Needed

Play Dates / Nanny Share

Menu / Bottles

Meal	Description / Time

Sleeps

Name: From: To:

☐ Check every 10 min

Expenses

Price	Description

Toileting / Nappies

Activities / Outings

SUNSCREEN ☐

Observations / Reflections

INITIAL

| MONDAY ☑ | TUESDAY ☐ | WEDNESDAY ☐ | THURSDAY ☐ | FRIDAY ☐ | SATURDAY ☐ | SUNDAY ☐ |

Our Day

DATE: START TIME: FINISH:

Family Communication to Nanny / Educator

Notes to Family / Supplies Needed

Play Dates / Nanny Share

Menu / Bottles
Meal	Description / Time

Sleeps
Name: From: To:

☐ Check every 10 min

Expenses
Price	Description

Toileting / Nappies

Activities / Outings

SUNSCREEN ☐

Observations / Reflections

INITIAL

MONDAY	TUESDAY	WEDNESDAY	THURSDAY	FRIDAY	SATURDAY	SUNDAY
☑	☐	☐	☐	☐	☐	☐

Our Day

DATE: START TIME: FINISH:

Family Communication to Nanny / Educator

Notes to Family / Supplies Needed

Play Dates / Nanny Share

Menu / Bottles

Meal	Description / Time

Sleeps

Name: From: To:

☐ Check every 10 min

Expenses

Price	Description

Toileting / Nappies

Activities / Outings

SUNSCREEN ☐

Observations / Reflections

INITIAL

| MONDAY ☑ | TUESDAY ☐ | WEDNESDAY ☐ | THURSDAY ☐ | FRIDAY ☐ | SATURDAY ☐ | SUNDAY ☐ |

Our Day

DATE: START TIME: FINISH:

Family Communication to Nanny / Educator

Notes to Family / Supplies Needed

Play Dates / Nanny Share

Menu / Bottles

Meal	Description / Time

Sleeps

Name: From: To:

☐ Check every 10 min

Expenses

Price	Description

Toileting / Nappies

Activities / Outings

SUNSCREEN ☐

Observations / Reflections

INITIAL

| MONDAY ☑ | TUESDAY ☐ | WEDNESDAY ☐ | THURSDAY ☐ | FRIDAY ☐ | SATURDAY ☐ | SUNDAY ☐ |

Our Day

DATE: START TIME: FINISH:

Family Communication to Nanny / Educator

Notes to Family / Supplies Needed

Play Dates / Nanny Share

Menu / Bottles
Meal | Description / Time

Sleeps
Name: From: To:

☐ Check every 10 min

Expenses
Price | Description

Toileting / Nappies

Activities / Outings
☐ SUNSCREEN

Observations / Reflections

INITIAL

© Butler Diaries

Our Day

| MONDAY ☑ | TUESDAY ☐ | WEDNESDAY ☐ | THURSDAY ☐ | FRIDAY ☐ | SATURDAY ☐ | SUNDAY ☐ |

DATE: START TIME: FINISH:

Family Communication to Nanny / Educator

Notes to Family / Supplies Needed

Play Dates / Nanny Share

Menu / Bottles

Meal	Description / Time

Sleeps

Name:	From:	To:

☐ Check every 10 min

Expenses

Price	Description

Toileting / Nappies

Activities / Outings

SUNSCREEN ☐

Observations / Reflections

INITIAL

| MONDAY ☑ | TUESDAY ☐ | WEDNESDAY ☐ | THURSDAY ☐ | FRIDAY ☐ | SATURDAY ☐ | SUNDAY ☐ |

Our Day

DATE: START TIME: FINISH:

Family Communication to Nanny / Educator

Notes to Family / Supplies Needed

Play Dates / Nanny Share

Menu / Bottles
Meal | Description / Time

Sleeps
Name: From: To:

☐ Check every 10 min

Expenses
Price | Description

Toileting / Nappies

Activities / Outings

SUNSCREEN ☐

Observations / Reflections

INITIAL

© Butler Diaries

Our Day

☑ MONDAY ☐ TUESDAY ☐ WEDNESDAY ☐ THURSDAY ☐ FRIDAY ☐ SATURDAY ☐ SUNDAY

DATE: START TIME: FINISH:

Family Communication to Nanny / Educator

Notes to Family / Supplies Needed

Play Dates / Nanny Share

Menu / Bottles
Meal	Description / Time

Sleeps
Name: From: To:

☐ Check every 10 min

Expenses
Price	Description

Toileting / Nappies

Activities / Outings

☐ SUNSCREEN

Observations / Reflections

INITIAL

© Butler Diaries

| MONDAY ☑ | TUESDAY ☐ | WEDNESDAY ☐ | THURSDAY ☐ | FRIDAY ☐ | SATURDAY ☐ | SUNDAY ☐ |

Our Day

DATE: START TIME: FINISH:

Family Communication to Nanny / Educator

Notes to Family / Supplies Needed

Play Dates / Nanny Share

Menu / Bottles

Meal	Description / Time

Sleeps

Name: From: To:

☐ Check every 10 min

Expenses

Price	Description

Toileting / Nappies

Activities / Outings

☐ SUNSCREEN

Observations / Reflections

INITIAL

© Butler Diaries

| MONDAY ☑ | TUESDAY ☐ | WEDNESDAY ☐ | THURSDAY ☐ | FRIDAY ☐ | SATURDAY ☐ | SUNDAY ☐ |

Our Day

DATE: START TIME: FINISH:

Family Communication to Nanny / Educator

Notes to Family / Supplies Needed

Play Dates / Nanny Share

Menu / Bottles

Meal	Description / Time

Sleeps

Name: From: To:

☐ Check every 10 min

Expenses

Price	Description

Toileting / Nappies

Activities / Outings

SUNSCREEN ☐

Observations / Reflections

INITIAL

© Butter Diaries

Our Day

MONDAY	TUESDAY	WEDNESDAY	THURSDAY	FRIDAY	SATURDAY	SUNDAY
☑	☐	☐	☐	☐	☐	☐

DATE: START TIME: FINISH:

Family Communication to Nanny / Educator

Notes to Family / Supplies Needed

Play Dates / Nanny Share

Menu / Bottles

Meal	Description / Time

Sleeps

Name: From: To:

☐ Check every 10 min

Expenses

Price	Description

Toileting / Nappies

Activities / Outings

SUNSCREEN ☐

Observations / Reflections

INITIAL

© Butler Diaries

| MONDAY ☑ | TUESDAY ☐ | WEDNESDAY ☐ | THURSDAY ☐ | FRIDAY ☐ | SATURDAY ☐ | SUNDAY ☐ |

Our Day

DATE: START TIME: FINISH:

Family Communication to Nanny / Educator

Notes to Family / Supplies Needed

Play Dates / Nanny Share

Menu / Bottles

Meal	Description / Time

Sleeps

Name: From: To:

☐ Check every 10 min

Expenses

Price	Description

Toileting / Nappies

Activities / Outings

SUNSCREEN ☐

Observations / Reflections

INITIAL

MONDAY	TUESDAY	WEDNESDAY	THURSDAY	FRIDAY	SATURDAY	SUNDAY
☑	☐	☐	☐	☐	☐	☐

Our Day

DATE: START TIME: FINISH:

Family Communication to Nanny / Educator

Notes to Family / Supplies Needed

Play Dates / Nanny Share

Menu / Bottles
Meal	Description / Time

Sleeps
Name: From: To:

☐ Check every 10 min

Expenses
Price	Description

Toileting / Nappies

Activities / Outings

SUNSCREEN ☐

Observations / Reflections

INITIAL

© Butler Diaries

| MONDAY ☑ | TUESDAY ☐ | WEDNESDAY ☐ | THURSDAY ☐ | FRIDAY ☐ | SATURDAY ☐ | SUNDAY ☐ |

Our Day

DATE:　　　　　　START TIME:　　　　　　FINISH:

Family Communication to Nanny / Educator

Notes to Family / Supplies Needed

Play Dates / Nanny Share

Menu / Bottles
Meal	Description / Time

Sleeps
Name:　　From:　　To:

☐ Check every 10 min

Expenses
Price	Description

Toileting / Nappies

Activities / Outings
SUNSCREEN ☐

Observations / Reflections

INITIAL

MONDAY	TUESDAY	WEDNESDAY	THURSDAY	FRIDAY	SATURDAY	SUNDAY
☑	☐	☐	☐	☐	☐	☐

Our Day

DATE: START TIME: FINISH:

Family Communication to Nanny / Educator

Notes to Family / Supplies Needed

Play Dates / Nanny Share

Menu / Bottles
Meal | Description / Time

Sleeps
Name: From: To:

☐ Check every 10 min

Expenses
Price | Description

Toileting / Nappies

Activities / Outings
☐ SUNSCREEN

Observations / Reflections

INITIAL

© Butler Diaries

Our Day

| MONDAY ☑ | TUESDAY ☐ | WEDNESDAY ☐ | THURSDAY ☐ | FRIDAY ☐ | SATURDAY ☐ | SUNDAY ☐ |

DATE: START TIME: FINISH:

Family Communication to Nanny / Educator

Notes to Family / Supplies Needed

Play Dates / Nanny Share

Menu / Bottles

Meal	Description / Time

Sleeps

Name: From: To:

☐ Check every 10 min

Expenses

Price	Description

Toileting / Nappies

Activities / Outings

SUNSCREEN ☐

Observations / Reflections

INITIAL

Our Day

| MONDAY ☑ | TUESDAY ☐ | WEDNESDAY ☐ | THURSDAY ☐ | FRIDAY ☐ | SATURDAY ☐ | SUNDAY ☐ |

DATE: START TIME: FINISH:

Family Communication to Nanny / Educator

Notes to Family / Supplies Needed

Play Dates / Nanny Share

Menu / Bottles
Meal	Description / Time

Sleeps
Name: From: To:

☐ Check every 10 min

Expenses
Price	Description

Toileting / Nappies

Activities / Outings

SUNSCREEN ☐

Observations / Reflections

INITIAL

© Butler Diaries

Our Day

| MONDAY ☑ | TUESDAY ☐ | WEDNESDAY ☐ | THURSDAY ☐ | FRIDAY ☐ | SATURDAY ☐ | SUNDAY ☐ |

DATE: START TIME: FINISH:

Family Communication to Nanny / Educator

Notes to Family / Supplies Needed

Play Dates / Nanny Share

Menu / Bottles

Meal	Description / Time

Sleeps

Name: From: To:

☐ Check every 10 min

Expenses

Price	Description

Toileting / Nappies

Activities / Outings

SUNSCREEN ☐

Observations / Reflections

INITIAL

Our Day

| MONDAY ☑ | TUESDAY ☐ | WEDNESDAY ☐ | THURSDAY ☐ | FRIDAY ☐ | SATURDAY ☐ | SUNDAY ☐ |

DATE: START TIME: FINISH:

Family Communication to Nanny / Educator

Notes to Family / Supplies Needed

Play Dates / Nanny Share

Menu / Bottles
Meal | Description / Time

Sleeps
Name: From: To:

☐ Check every 10 min

Expenses
Price | Description

Toileting / Nappies

Activities / Outings

SUNSCREEN ☐

Observations / Reflections

INITIAL

© Butler Diaries

| MONDAY ☑ | TUESDAY ☐ | WEDNESDAY ☐ | THURSDAY ☐ | FRIDAY ☐ | SATURDAY ☐ | SUNDAY ☐ |

Our Day

DATE: START TIME: FINISH:

Family Communication to Nanny / Educator

Notes to Family / Supplies Needed

Play Dates / Nanny Share

Menu / Bottles

Meal	Description / Time

Sleeps

Name: From: To:

☐ Check every 10 min

Expenses

Price	Description

Toileting / Nappies

Activities / Outings

SUNSCREEN ☐

Observations / Reflections

INITIAL

© Butter Diaries

| MONDAY ☑ | TUESDAY ☐ | WEDNESDAY ☐ | THURSDAY ☐ | FRIDAY ☐ | SATURDAY ☐ | SUNDAY ☐ |

Our Day

DATE:　　　　　　START TIME:　　　　　　FINISH:

Family Communication to Nanny / Educator

Notes to Family / Supplies Needed

Play Dates / Nanny Share

Menu / Bottles

Meal	Description / Time

Sleeps

Name:　　From:　　To:

☐ Check every 10 min

Expenses

Price	Description

Toileting / Nappies

Activities / Outings

☐ SUNSCREEN

Observations / Reflections

INITIAL

© Butler Diaries

| MONDAY ☑ | TUESDAY ☐ | WEDNESDAY ☐ | THURSDAY ☐ | FRIDAY ☐ | SATURDAY ☐ | SUNDAY ☐ |

Our Day

DATE: START TIME: FINISH:

Family Communication to Nanny / Educator

Notes to Family / Supplies Needed

Play Dates / Nanny Share

Menu / Bottles

Meal	Description / Time

Sleeps

Name: From: To:

☐ Check every 10 min

Expenses

Price	Description

Toileting / Nappies

Activities / Outings

SUNSCREEN ☐

Observations / Reflections

INITIAL

© Butter Diaries

Our Day

MONDAY	TUESDAY	WEDNESDAY	THURSDAY	FRIDAY	SATURDAY	SUNDAY
☑	☐	☐	☐	☐	☐	☐

DATE: START TIME: FINISH:

Family Communication to Nanny / Educator

Notes to Family / Supplies Needed

Play Dates / Nanny Share

Menu / Bottles

Meal	Description / Time

Sleeps

Name:	From:	To:

☐ Check every 10 min

Expenses

Price	Description

Toileting / Nappies

Activities / Outings

☐ SUNSCREEN

Observations / Reflections

INITIAL

© Butler Diaries

Our Day

| MONDAY ☑ | TUESDAY ☐ | WEDNESDAY ☐ | THURSDAY ☐ | FRIDAY ☐ | SATURDAY ☐ | SUNDAY ☐ |

DATE: START TIME: FINISH:

Family Communication to Nanny / Educator

Notes to Family / Supplies Needed

Play Dates / Nanny Share

Menu / Bottles

Meal	Description / Time

Sleeps

Name: From: To:

☐ Check every 10 min

Expenses

Price	Description

Toileting / Nappies

Activities / Outings

SUNSCREEN ☐

Observations / Reflections

INITIAL

© Butler Diaries

| MONDAY ☑ | TUESDAY ☐ | WEDNESDAY ☐ | THURSDAY ☐ | FRIDAY ☐ | SATURDAY ☐ | SUNDAY ☐ |

Our Day

DATE: START TIME: FINISH:

Family Communication to Nanny / Educator

Notes to Family / Supplies Needed

Play Dates / Nanny Share

Menu / Bottles
Meal	Description / Time

Sleeps
Name: From: To:

☐ Check every 10 min

Expenses
Price	Description

Toileting / Nappies

Activities / Outings

SUNSCREEN ☐

Observations / Reflections

INITIAL

© Butler Diaries

| MONDAY ☑ | TUESDAY ☐ | WEDNESDAY ☐ | THURSDAY ☐ | FRIDAY ☐ | SATURDAY ☐ | SUNDAY ☐ |

Our Day

DATE:　　　　　　　START TIME:　　　　　　　FINISH:

Family Communication to Nanny / Educator

Notes to Family / Supplies Needed

Play Dates / Nanny Share

Menu / Bottles
Meal	Description / Time

Sleeps
Name:　　From:　　To:

☐ Check every 10 min

Expenses
Price	Description

Toileting / Nappies

Activities / Outings

SUNSCREEN ☐

Observations / Reflections

INITIAL

© Butter Diaries

| MONDAY ☑ | TUESDAY ☐ | WEDNESDAY ☐ | THURSDAY ☐ | FRIDAY ☐ | SATURDAY ☐ | SUNDAY ☐ |

Our Day

DATE: START TIME: FINISH:

Family Communication to Nanny / Educator

Notes to Family / Supplies Needed

Play Dates / Nanny Share

Menu / Bottles
Meal	Description / Time

Sleeps
Name:	From:	To:

☐ Check every 10 min

Expenses
Price	Description

Toileting / Nappies

Activities / Outings

SUNSCREEN ☐

Observations / Reflections

INITIAL

© Butler Diaries

Our Day

| MONDAY ☑ | TUESDAY ☐ | WEDNESDAY ☐ | THURSDAY ☐ | FRIDAY ☐ | SATURDAY ☐ | SUNDAY ☐ |

DATE: START TIME: FINISH:

Family Communication to Nanny / Educator

Notes to Family / Supplies Needed

Play Dates / Nanny Share

Menu / Bottles

Meal	Description / Time

Sleeps

Name: From: To:

☐ Check every 10 min

Expenses

Price	Description

Toileting / Nappies

Activities / Outings

SUNSCREEN ☐

Observations / Reflections

INITIAL

© Butter Diaries

Our Day

| MONDAY ☑ | TUESDAY ☐ | WEDNESDAY ☐ | THURSDAY ☐ | FRIDAY ☐ | SATURDAY ☐ | SUNDAY ☐ |

DATE: START TIME: FINISH:

Family Communication to Nanny / Educator

Notes to Family / Supplies Needed

Play Dates / Nanny Share

Menu / Bottles

Meal	Description / Time

Sleeps

Name: From: To:

☐ Check every 10 min

Expenses

Price	Description

Toileting / Nappies

Activities / Outings

SUNSCREEN ☐

Observations / Reflections

INITIAL

© Butler Diaries

| MONDAY ☑ | TUESDAY ☐ | WEDNESDAY ☐ | THURSDAY ☐ | FRIDAY ☐ | SATURDAY ☐ | SUNDAY ☐ |

Our Day

DATE: START TIME: FINISH:

Family Communication to Nanny / Educator

Notes to Family / Supplies Needed

Play Dates / Nanny Share

Menu / Bottles
| Meal | Description / Time |

Sleeps
Name: From: To:

☐ Check every 10 min

Expenses
| Price | Description |

Toileting / Nappies

Activities / Outings

SUNSCREEN ☐

Observations / Reflections

INITIAL

© Butler Diaries

MONDAY	TUESDAY	WEDNESDAY	THURSDAY	FRIDAY	SATURDAY	SUNDAY
☑ ☐	☐	☐	☐	☐	☐	☐

Our Day

DATE: START TIME: FINISH:

Family Communication to Nanny / Educator

Notes to Family / Supplies Needed

Play Dates / Nanny Share

Menu / Bottles
Meal	Description / Time

Sleeps
Name: From: To:

☐ Check every 10 min

Expenses
Price	Description

Toileting / Nappies

Activities / Outings

SUNSCREEN ☐

Observations / Reflections

INITIAL

Our Day

☑ MONDAY ☐ TUESDAY ☐ WEDNESDAY ☐ THURSDAY ☐ FRIDAY ☐ SATURDAY ☐ SUNDAY

DATE: START TIME: FINISH:

Family Communication to Nanny / Educator

Notes to Family / Supplies Needed

Play Dates / Nanny Share

Menu / Bottles

Meal	Description / Time

Sleeps

Name: From: To:

☐ Check every 10 min

Expenses

Price	Description

Toileting / Nappies

Activities / Outings

☐ SUNSCREEN

Observations / Reflections

INITIAL

Our Day

| MONDAY ☑ | TUESDAY ☐ | WEDNESDAY ☐ | THURSDAY ☐ | FRIDAY ☐ | SATURDAY ☐ | SUNDAY ☐ |

DATE: START TIME: FINISH:

Family Communication to Nanny / Educator

Notes to Family / Supplies Needed

Play Dates / Nanny Share

Menu / Bottles

Meal	Description / Time

Sleeps

Name: From: To:

☐ Check every 10 min

Expenses

Price	Description

Toileting / Nappies

Activities / Outings

SUNSCREEN ☐

Observations / Reflections

INITIAL

© Butler Diaries

Our Day

MONDAY	TUESDAY	WEDNESDAY	THURSDAY	FRIDAY	SATURDAY	SUNDAY
☑	☐	☐	☐	☐	☐	☐

DATE: START TIME: FINISH:

Family Communication to Nanny / Educator

Notes to Family / Supplies Needed

Play Dates / Nanny Share

Menu / Bottles

Meal	Description / Time

Sleeps

Name: From: To:

☐ Check every 10 min

Expenses

Price	Description

Toileting / Nappies

Activities / Outings

SUNSCREEN ☐

Observations / Reflections

INITIAL

© Butter Diaries

| MONDAY ☑ | TUESDAY ☐ | WEDNESDAY ☐ | THURSDAY ☐ | FRIDAY ☐ | SATURDAY ☐ | SUNDAY ☐ |

Our Day

DATE: START TIME: FINISH:

Family Communication to Nanny / Educator

Notes to Family / Supplies Needed

Play Dates / Nanny Share

Menu / Bottles
Meal	Description / Time

Sleeps
Name: From: To:

☐ Check every 10 min

Expenses
Price	Description

Toileting / Nappies

Activities / Outings

SUNSCREEN ☐

Observations / Reflections

INITIAL

Our Day

| MONDAY ☑ | TUESDAY ☐ | WEDNESDAY ☐ | THURSDAY ☐ | FRIDAY ☐ | SATURDAY ☐ | SUNDAY ☐ |

DATE: START TIME: FINISH:

Family Communication to Nanny / Educator

Notes to Family / Supplies Needed

Play Dates / Nanny Share

Menu / Bottles

Meal	Description / Time

Sleeps

Name: From: To:

☐ Check every 10 min

Expenses

Price	Description

Toileting / Nappies

Activities / Outings

SUNSCREEN ☐

Observations / Reflections

INITIAL

© Butter Diaries

| MONDAY ☑ | TUESDAY ☐ | WEDNESDAY ☐ | THURSDAY ☐ | FRIDAY ☐ | SATURDAY ☐ | SUNDAY ☐ |

Our Day

DATE: START TIME: FINISH:

Family Communication to Nanny / Educator

Notes to Family / Supplies Needed

Play Dates / Nanny Share

Menu / Bottles

Meal	Description / Time

Sleeps

Name: From: To:

☐ Check every 10 min

Expenses

Price	Description

Toileting / Nappies

Activities / Outings

SUNSCREEN ☐

Observations / Reflections

INITIAL

| MONDAY ☑ | TUESDAY ☐ | WEDNESDAY ☐ | THURSDAY ☐ | FRIDAY ☐ | SATURDAY ☐ | SUNDAY ☐ |

Our Day

DATE: START TIME: FINISH:

Family Communication to Nanny / Educator

Notes to Family / Supplies Needed

Play Dates / Nanny Share

Menu / Bottles
Meal	Description / Time

Sleeps
Name: From: To:

☐ Check every 10 min

Expenses
Price	Description

Toileting / Nappies

Activities / Outings   SUNSCREEN ☐

Observations / Reflections

INITIAL

© Butler Diaries

SPACE FOR NOTES

www.ingramcontent.com/pod-product-compliance
Lightning Source LLC
Chambersburg PA
CBHW060501240426
43661CB00006B/877